Telemarketer's Revenge: The Customer Is Always Wrong, Bitch!

SIDNEY S. PRASAD

Copyright © 2013 Sidney S. Prasad

All rights reserved.

ISBN:1927676258
ISBN-13: 978-1-927676-25-7

DEDICATION

This book is dedicated to the late Mr. and Mrs. Ram Lakhan, my dear grandparents. You witnessed my arrival into your family and were always there for me. And I was there for you to say goodbye when you left this world. Both of you wrote a phenomenal manuscript for your lives and I thank you for including me in it, especially in your final chapters. I'm pretty confident that if you were alive today, you would kick my ass for writing trashy novels, so I waited till you were gone to publish them.

CONTENTS

	Acknowledgments	i
1	The Customer Is Always Wrong, Bitch!	1
2	Murder, She Wrote	13
3	Foreign Porn Sucks!	23
4	Fuck The Competition	35
5	Pooper Scooper	45
6	Brainiac Parents vs. Dumb Kids	53
7	Dumb Ass!	64
8	Crying Wolf	75
9	Curious Critters	83
10	Come In And Shit Down	93

ACKNOWLEDGMENTS

Hi! My name is Sidney Prasad, and I enjoy bugging the shit out of people for a living! I take my hat off to all those beautiful men and women who are employed in the field of selling! I deeply applaud anyone out there who has to deal with the general public for a living.

The truth of the matter is we don't have the luxury of hiding behind a machine in a factory or a beam on a construction site. Unfortunately, we have a phone stuck to our ear for eight hours a day. We are sort of jaded in life, sentenced to listening to nagging, chronic, pathological lying customers vocalizing their shit as we kiss their fat ass for a couple of measly dollars.

Whether someone hangs up on us or tells us where to go, it's kind of satisfying knowing that our thirty-second phone call just ruined their dinner and their miserable existence. No matter what people hypothesize about the field of selling, it's the greatest profession in the world!

Statistically speaking, five percent of all self-made millionaires in America are sales professionals. Every time someone tells a salesperson to eff off, they don't realize it, but they're helping to build our character. Telemarketers have heard every excuse in the book and have been sworn at in almost every language in the world.

All the rejection and negativity that we have absorbed has translated into abundant confidence. In the modern age of online dating, people often complain that they are never approached by anyone on the street anymore. That's not the case for salespeople, as we have the skills and confidence to go after anything and anyone that we want! I wrote this book to give all my brothers and sisters in the field of serving the public the respect they so badly deserve.

I'm not in any way suggesting you try any of the tactics in this book, as some schemes could be illegal and very immoral. But I want to make my readers laugh and imagine if the tables were turned and, one day, telemarketers got their revenge!

1 THE CUSTOMER IS ALWAYS WRONG, BITCH!

I strongly feel that society has programmed the wrong information into potential consumers. The most loosely thrown around phrase is, "the customer is always right," which is a complete crock of shit! Saying "the customer is always right" has given false empowerment to potential consumers, making these nobodies feel like they're somebody. Just because someone is a prospect doesn't give them the right to treat telemarketers like shit.

If people could just look inside themselves, they would realize that they are responsible for their own problems. But instead, society decides as a whole to negatively displace their anger and frustrations on poor defenseless telemarketers. Door-to-door salesmen, retail salespeople, and telemarketers are people, too, and genuinely understand when someone is not interested. But society chooses to take their sexual frustrations out on innocent salespeople and insult them.

Why can't mankind just be blatantly honest and say, "Look sir, your product or service doesn't suit my needs, and I feel that I'm not an eligible candidate." That would be enough to convince most decent salespeople to end the call and move on to the next prospect.

"A hypocrite is someone who claims that they don't do business on the phone and then calls Pizza Hut to order dinner."

—Sidney S. Prasad

One day, veteran telemarketer Jack Goff decided to solicit Lou Zar regarding chimney-sweep services. Rather than being honest with the telemarketer and just admitting he is a deadbeat and doesn't own a chimney or a Hibachi, Lou Zar said, "Good going, asshole. You made me drop coffee on my nuts. Hold on a minute while I grab some rubbing alcohol."

A minute later, Lou Zar came back and mentioned that he was rubbing some alcohol on his nuts, and then started screaming violently that his nuts were burning! The chilling screams of discomfort prompted telemarketer Jack Goff to end the call.

Telemarketers have heard every excuse in the book and can appreciate a creative, innovative bullshit story. Now Jack Goff can't verify if the prospect did indeed drop coffee on his private parts. But he can verify that he is pissed off at the way Lou Zar treated him. The majority of prospects fail to realize what kind of maniacs they are pissing off every time they swear, bullshit, or hang up on poor telemarketers. Why are consumers so ignorant, you ask? Because customers think they are protected by that false-charter "the customer is always right" b.s.

TELEMARKETER'S REVENGE: THE CUSTOMER IS ALWAYS WRONG, BITCH!

After listening to Lou Zar's response, Jack Goff's gut instinct was to go over to his house and hang a "Do Not Disturb, Intensely Masturbating" sign on his door. But Jack Goff realized he wanted to take it a bit further than that. Since Lou Zar claimed that he burnt his nuts with coffee, Uncle Jack is going to help him out by creating an online profile for him on a transsexual dating website. Jack Goff is pretty confident that Lou Zar will get contacted by some freak who can rub alcohol on his nuts in a comforting manner, because the customer is always right!

"Does everybody answer the phone when they are having sex?"

—Sidney S. Prasad

WHY DO THEY ANSWER THE PHONE?

Most seasoned telemarketers turn their phones off or don't answer them when they are enjoying their downtime. That's a pretty simple concept, don't you think? But on the other side of the fence, telemarketers can't fathom why people answer the phone when they're so-called busy. If a prospect is busy watching a re-run of *Seinfeld*, then enjoy the show, don't answer the phone, and treat the poor salesperson like they're Newman.

Robin Banks was the owner-operator of a computer tutorial company and decided to market the company with a telephone campaign. One day, he called up an eligible prospect named Ryan Coke and promoted his services. Ryan Coke claimed that he didn't feel comfortable doing business on the phone and got rid of Robin Banks by asking him to email some literature. A week later, Robin Banks gave Ryan Coke a follow-up call on the email. Ryan Coke said he couldn't access his email, as he isn't too computer savvy and doesn't really know how to use a computer too well.

"You're considered a snob if you ignore the greeter at Walmart and you're considered an asshole if you hang up on a telemarketer."

—Sidney S. Prasad

TELEMARKETER'S REVENGE: THE CUSTOMER IS ALWAYS WRONG, BITCH!

Robin Banks was fuming at this point, due to the penis-head that just pulled a fast one on him. Robin Banks noticed that the email didn't bounce back and was a valid email address, so obviously Ryan Coke was full of shit. Robin Banks really wanted to go over and pour sugar in Ryan Coke's gas tank, but that wasn't satisfying enough. Since Ryan Coke prefers regular postal mail to email, Robin Banks decided to write a letter to Ryan Coke, pretending that it was from a local hospital. The letter explained that one of Ryan Coke's former lovers just got diagnosed with a severe sexually transmitted disease and was worried Ryan Coke might have been infected and to get tested right away.

"Roses are red, violets are blue, just say you're not interested so I can hang up on you!"

—Sidney S. Prasad

911 IS A JOKE

What's that old expression? Something like "money talks and bullshit walks?" It's bad enough that salespeople are portrayed as fast-talking, con-artist criminals. But what about the customers? If anything, they bullshit more than all of us in the boiler room. I'm quite confident when a prospect tells a telemarketer that they're busy, they are actually busy with their thumb up their ass. On the sales side, it's considered negative behavior for salespeople to bitch about lying prospects.

While consulting for a stationery supply company, Rick O'Shee decided to call on a beauty school in hopes of selling some office supplies to them. His opening pitch got interrupted within a few seconds by Anita Fixx, the prospect who answered the phone. Anita Fixx claimed that one of the students fainted and they were waiting for an ambulance. Empathetically, Rick O'Shee excused Anita Fixx and rescheduled the call.

"What do you need to sleep on? It's a $2.95 long distance plan."

—Sidney S. Prasad

TELEMARKETER'S REVENGE: THE CUSTOMER IS ALWAYS WRONG, BITCH!

Two weeks later, Rick O'Shee attempted to call the same beauty school, and guess what happened? Anita Fixx answered the phone and rudely interrupted Rick O'Shee before he could make the pitch with the exact same ambulance excuse. Rick O'Shee felt like he got bamboozled. He shared the embarrassing story with a colleague of his, Dinah Soares, who told him Anita Fixx was her cousin and that's her favorite excuse to escape sales calls.

If this were Rick O'Shee's roommate, the revenge would be really easy by just merely pissing in Anita Fixx's mouthwash, as this would even the score. Rick O'Shee decided to be patient and waited for the coldest day of the year during a -40°C blizzard. Then, he called the police from a payphone and said there was a bomb in the beauty school. Naturally, the police had to investigate, and everyone was outside for a couple of hours in the cold until the perimeter was secure.

"I'm doing fine; thank you for not asking!"

—Sidney S. Prasad

ARE YOU CAMERA-SHY?

In my personal humble opinion, I think the people who lie to salespeople are pretty stupid. Do prospects actually think that the salesperson believes them when they say they are busy or they purchased the product being pitched a week ago? Consumers fail to realize the mathematics of selling, where sales professionals usually have to hear a few dozen declines before someone actually buys something. For every prospect that rejects them, there is a sappy story to go with it, and salespeople have heard every excuse in the book. But they do appreciate an original, innovative white lie, as it makes a great drinking story.

Sue Flay, a sales representative for a portrait studio, decided to call some leads. She phoned up Dick Hunter's residence and attempted to pitch him on some family portraits. The background sounded like he was hosting a wife-swapping party or something. It was just too noisy for a typical board-game-and-root-beer party. Dick Hunter declined Sue Flay's offer of a limited time $24.95 family portrait special. Dick Hunter requested a callback in ten years. His justification for the extended time lag was that he had just been handed a ten-year prison sentence for mismanaging a daycare and would be off to jail shortly.

"I'm sorry, I didn't mean to wake you up, Ma'am. It's only, like, two o'clock in the afternoon! My bad!"

—Sidney S. Prasad

TELEMARKETER'S REVENGE: THE CUSTOMER IS ALWAYS WRONG, BITCH!

Immediately after the call, Sue Flay slammed her fists on the desk because she knew the guy was lying but she was impressed with Dick's creativity. If she had access to his house, then she would sneak into his bathroom and pour Nair hair remover into his shampoo. This would cause the guy to wait a couple of years before his eyebrows grow back. But life is not that easy, as she didn't own any lock picks.

However, Sue Flay — and pretty much anyone else — could have access to the outside of Dick Hunter's house. Sue Flay decided to get even by putting a large sign on Dick Hunter's lawn. The sign read, in big bold letters, "Beware, A Pedophile Lives Here."

"Have you ever thought about trading in one of your ugly children for an answering machine? At least this way, it will take messages for the calls that you don't want!"

—Sidney S. Prasad

IMPERSONATIONS SUCK!

In the field of selling, we are taught that the average upset customer will tell ten people about their negative experiences. But what customers fail to realize is that every salesperson that they shit on will go tell one hundred other salespeople about that particular client. Believe it or not, there are some salespeople who hold on to prospects' numbers who gave them shit or pissed them off. Then, they will purposely prank the prospect at 3:00 AM Saturday night after the nightclub and tell them to go fuck themselves.

That's actually letting the prospect off easy. Consumers don't realize that if they got someone fired or escalated, that salesperson will keep that consumer's name and number etched in their skull and will get even eventually. What does the salesperson have to lose, since they just lost their high-paying, seven-dollar-per-hour job? Think about it.

Daryl Rhea has been selling on the phone consistently for the last five years. He is acutely aware if he's talking too fast or too slow, and of when to close. One day, he attempted to sell some toilet bowl clogging insurance to Joe King. Joe King was pretty decent, as he listened to Daryl Rhea's pitch in its entirety and didn't interrupt him once.

TELEMARKETER'S REVENGE: THE CUSTOMER IS ALWAYS WRONG, BITCH!

"Why do people answer the phone if they are fucken' busy?"

—Sidney S. Prasad

After listening to Daryl Rhea's pitch, Joe King told Daryl Rhea that his company hired him randomly to audit Daryl Rhea and his teammates' telephone conduct. Joe King instructed Daryl to stand up during the next couple of phone calls to project his voice a little better. He also told Daryl Rhea not to pause as much, as it gives the prospect an opportunity to interject with some reluctance. Joe King concluded the call by telling Daryl Rhea that he wouldn't report him, and just to improve on the points discussed.

Daryl didn't care too much about Joe King's comments and had sex with his boss, Polly Ester, during his lunch break. He then asked Polly Ester if there was a random audit in place. Polly Ester just laughed. She explained to Daryl Rhea that it was a prank, and Joe King is full of so much shit that his eyes are brown.

Daryl Rhea was so pissed off that he wanted to rub dog shit on the door handles of Joe King's car and the doorknobs of his house, but he didn't want to stoop that low. So he picked up the phone and called the anonymous tax-fraud line and reported Joe King to the government, since he likes random audits so much. (This is illegal and punishable by law in most states, unless you have genuine suspicion that someone is defrauding the government)

"Karma is a bitch! I'm curious about what I did in my last life to be punished working for this asshole?"

—Sidney S. Prasad, My Bipolar Manager

2 MURDER, SHE WROTE

It's bad enough that prospects seriously believe that their shit don't stink. Worse, they truly still believe that the-customer-is-always-right bullshit. It chokes my chicken when I hear people come up with rehearsed schemes as comebacks to telemarketers. It's like, why can't friggin' consumers grow some nuts and just say they are not interested, rather than making the poor telemarketer jump through hoops in order to end the call?

Amateur telemarketer Doug Graves was employed at a lawn-care company, promoting yard maintenance services. One day, he phoned the residence of Dr. Wako Ho, and the man who picked up sounded like he was really sexually frustrated by the way he projected his voice. In the back of Doug Graves's mind, he was praying that he didn't interrupt the prospect while he was playing a friendly game of pocket pool because the referee's always a dick.

"Didn't your mother teach you it's rude to talk with your mouth full? Especially to telemarketers?"

—Sidney S. Prasad

Doug Graves started with his pitch by identifying who he was and what he was attempting to promote. All of a sudden, the man's voice changed as he asked Doug Graves for his full name and to hold on for a second. Doug Graves could hear the prospect yelling in the background, saying, "Okay, boys, get some close-up pictures of the body and weapon and then dust them for prints."

The prospect came back to the phone and identified himself as Sergeant Mike Hunt, who told Doug Graves that Dr. Wako Ho was no longer with us and that Doug just phoned a murder scene. To make it worse, Sergeant Mike Hunt cross-examined Doug Graves on the phone for the next half-hour, questioning his relationship with Dr. Wako Ho and refusing to accept that it was a random telemarketing call.

We can all agree that this is an awesome burn, as it made poor Doug Graves shit bricks for that painful half-hour while being questioned. Doug Graves wished he had the money and muscle to plant a whole crop of marijuana plants in that guy's backyard for what he did to him. But, obviously, he doesn't, certainly not on a telemarketer's salary. Plus, that's really cruel, because Dr. Wako Ho would probably end up sharing a jail cell with some nympho named Bubba when he got busted.

TELEMARKETER'S REVENGE: THE CUSTOMER IS ALWAYS WRONG, BITCH!

But since Dr. Wako Ho wanted to play hardball, Doug Graves could still give this loser a run for his money.

After work, Doug Graves went to his own car and slapped a big "For Sale sign" on his back window. The sale sign had Dr. Wako Ho's phone number and address on it. Then Doug Graves drove like an asshole for four hours around the city — cutting people off, tailgating cars, and giving people the finger — and then went home. Doug Graves is going to sleep like a baby, because it's Dr. Wako Ho's phone number and address on that sign.

"Order your date fish and you've fed her for the night. Teach her how to fish and you're not getting laid!"

—Sidney S. Prasad, My Bipolar Manager

BUYERS ARE LIARS!

In today's modern age of computers, most telemarketing firms equip their salespeople with computer software like Maximizer or Goldmine. This software allows the salespersons to document each call and its outcome. But the prospects, for some reason, think it's like *The Little Rascals*-era where they are being pitched by a telephone made out of soup cans and string. A good liar will stick to the same story until they believe its reality themselves. A bad liar will keep changing their excuses on why they can't afford a fucken' $2.95 long-distance plan.

Rose Bush was employed as a telemarketer for promoting coupon books for fetish parties and sex toys. She was going through her leads and decided to call up Pierce Cox. She figured this would be an easy sell because Pierce Cox had already been pitched about her company's promotions. Confidently, Rose Bush phoned up Pierce Cox to see if he would be interested in the coupon books, and he said to send him some information in the mail and ended the call.

"Don't you hate it when you are trying to rob a bank and the teller asks you if you are going to your 20-year high school reunion?"

—Sidney S. Prasad, Don't Ask Dumb Questions!

TELEMARKETER'S REVENGE: THE CUSTOMER IS ALWAYS WRONG, BITCH!

Now, here's where "buyers are liars" kicks in. Rose Bush checked the notes of all the previous calls and discovered that the prospect had been mailed literature five times. The sales industry is fully aware of "send it to me in the mail" as a sign of reluctance. It's a really nice way of telling the telemarketer to fuck off. There are a lot of companies that refuse to send shit in the mail, as it is just a waste of postage and time. From a telemarketer's perspective, it would be shitty and a double-whammy if you made a follow up call on the shit you sent in the mail and the prospect told you that they were fucken' illiterate.

If Pierce Cox were in arms' reach, I'm sure Rose Bush would have kicked him in the nuts until his jaws swelled. Rose Bush decided to give the prospect what he wanted. She ripped out several dozens of information-request forms out of magazines and catalogues. She filled in Pierce Cox's personal information, which will result in hundreds of catalogues, pamphlets, brochures, and all kinds of funky shit sent to Pierce Cox's residence to get even.

"I don't mean to pry, but I didn't hear the water running after you flushed the toilet. I don't like to assume things, but should I take it that you used sanitizer instead of washing your hands?"

—Sidney S. Prasad

EVERYONE IS A CHARITY

Holly Day was a telephone fundraiser for a local reputable children's charity. The first call that she made was to Mr. I.P. Freely. In her pitches, she stressed the importance of helping needy children, who have no other means of support. Mr. I.P. Freely decided to be a jerk, and respond by saying, "I hate children; I hate those little snot-nosed brats and wish they would all shit and die. I want to get in my car and run over all those little fuckers." Then he started laughing in a demented tone and continued the rant for a couple of minutes. Obviously, Holly Day doesn't want anything to do with this psycho or his money. She thanked him for his time and ended the call.

Holly Day's family didn't have cable growing up, so therefore she came from a big family with five sisters and four brothers. She really loved kids, and took the insult from Mr. I.P. Freely to heart. In a perfect world, she would call up and pay some Girl Guides and Cub Scouts to kick the shit out of this guy, but she was a little classier than that.

On her break, she phoned up twenty dentists and twenty other specialists and then made appointments on behalf of Mr. I.P. Freely. She made a point of only booking appointments with the seventy-five dollar no-show policy.

"Get you off what list? Santa's list? Craigslist?"

—Sidney S. Prasad

TELEMARKETER'S REVENGE: THE CUSTOMER IS ALWAYS WRONG, BITCH!

ECHOES

There is no better time to be living than this present moment. It makes me smile every time I enter a grocery store or mall and there is free sanitizer, like on every corner of this planet. If I want to treat myself to a really expensive meal in the food court or a ritzy fast-food drive-thru, I have the peace of mind knowing that the food handlers are wearing gloves. With the emergence of increasing sanitary conditions, I don't know why people throw all of that out the window and take the phone with them into the shitter. What, are they scared they are going to fall into the toilet and not be able to locate a log to hold onto?

Inside salespeople spend anywhere between twenty-five and forty-plus hours on the phone per week. We pick up everyone's bad habits, and we know when someone is gobbling down a couple of Big Macs while talking to us. What's even more disturbing is when we call upon residential clients and they are pushing out some steak and eggs with their ass cheeks while chatting with us.

Let me get this straight: Telemarketers don't have the luxury of making cold calls while on the shitter, but the consumer can get away with talking to us while they're having sex, beating their kids, and shitting out cornbread?

Telemarketers, the best way to settle the score with these degenerates is to schedule an automatic callback every two minutes and don't let that prospect take their shit in peace. Then, wait about half an hour and call from the payphone in the lunchroom and say, "So how was it?"

"God loves you! Especially when you're talking to a telemarketer and the other line goes off."

—Sidney S. Prasad

TELEMARKETER'S REVENGE: THE CUSTOMER IS ALWAYS WRONG, BITCH!

INAPPROPRIATELY FUNNY

Honesty is the best policy in most circumstances. Salespeople throughout time — past, present and future — will always be left to wonder why prospects behave the way they do. Going into the field, telemarketers are pre-warned that the majority of the calls will end up with people hanging up and the occasionally cursing and screaming fit. But if telemarketers are deemed crazy for calling the client during dinner, how about the clients' behavior? "Oh, sorry, Mr. Customer! Did I make you miss your turn when the can of Chef Boyardee was getting passed around at dinner?"

The whole sales process could be a lot more painless if prospects were just blatantly honest. Salespeople wish that prospects would come straight out and say; "Listen, I'm a fucken' deadbeat living off food stamps and Kraft dinner and can't afford your $3.99 magazine subscription." Instead, prospects tend to be snarly about it and have air-horns and noisemakers by the phone to spring on a defenseless telemarketer. Or they take their phone to the toilet and flush it a couple of times with the phone next to it for the telemarketer to interpret that they are not interested.

"My sales manager couldn't sell shit to a toilet paper factory if his life depended on it!"

—Sidney S. Prasad, My Bipolar Manager

One day, rookie telemarketer April Shours made the first call of her shift to a gentleman named Gaye Barr. When the phone rang, Gaye Barr was busy slaving away in the kitchen, attempting to cook a one-course gourmet meal that consisted of a can of soup. Gaye Barr was hoping it was his date, Luke Warm, reporting that he was running fashionably late. This would give Gaye Barr enough time to run next door and bum some crackers off his neighbor's bird.

Gaye Barr answered the phone and said, "Hi, Luke," but was disappointed when April Shours started pitching a magazine subscription. Gaye Barr thought about April Shours' pitch for about two seconds. He decided that between the mouthwash jug and the shampoo bottle, he's got enough reading material in the shitter to last him a year. He also remembered his boyfriend Luke Warm left his *Playgirl* magazine collection for him to read. Rather than being decent about declining April Shours, Gaye Barr stuck the phone next to the blender for a couple of minutes until April Shours hung up.

If Gaye Barr was April Shours' neighbor, she would climb through the bathroom window and put Saran Wrap on his toilet. Unfortunately, life isn't that easy, and April lived on the other side of town. But she was certain she would get even, so she called up Gaye Barr's apartment manager and got his contact information. April Shours then drafted a phony eviction letter, impersonating Gaye Barr's landlord, and sent it to him.

"Did you ever wonder why unemployed people and welfare recipients never get to be contestants on game shows? Because they could really use the fucken' money!"

—Sidney S. Prasad, My Bipolar Manager

3 FOREIGN PORN SUCKS!

Salespeople all across the board tolerate all levels of childish abuse from their prospects. It's one thing for the consumer to be a jerk and beat around the bush rather than say they are not interested, but it's another thing to use technology to insult the salesperson. This takes me to a tale involving a sales representative, Rhea Curran, who called upon Jay Walker.

Jay Walker, like most men of the twenty-first century, had lost his mojo in the Nineties and was dependent upon online dating websites. Jay Walker was also aware that most girls block their phone numbers when calling a potential blind date the first time. Like a sassy little schoolboy, Jay Walker was sitting next to the phone, waiting for it to ring. Jay Walker was hoping it was this chick that he was emailing back and forth named Sally Snatch, but instead it was Rhea Curran.

Rhea Curran pitched Jay Walker on some gutter-cleaning services. Jay Walker thought this was a true waste of his time because he lived in a rental and Mr. Roper took care of cleaning the gutters. Rather than kindly explaining to Rhea Curran that he rents a slum in the ghetto and doesn't own a home, Jay Walker decided to get cocky and blast foreign porn off the Internet into the phone until Rhea Curran hung up.

"You sound pretty tough on the phone; I dare you to say this to me in person! Oh yeah, I know where you live: 6969 Sex Drive."

—Sidney S. Prasad

Rhea Curran's gut instincts told her to dip Jay Walker's toothbrush into the toilet. But unfortunately that toothbrush wasn't in arm's reach. She took a breather and thought about it. Since Jay Walker thinks he is cool and an alpha-male wannabe, then let's send him some love! Rhea Curran called up a dozen different flower shops and had some really expensive bouquets delivered to Jay Walker's house with explicit instructions: cash on delivery.

"Here's a challenge: order a pizza and then call 911. See who gets there first."

—Sidney S. Prasad

TELEMARKETER'S REVENGE: THE CUSTOMER IS ALWAYS WRONG, BITCH!

PRIVATE PARTS

The beauty of being employed in the field of sales is you come across all walks of life and personality types. One of the delicate hurdles salespeople face is insecure spouses. One of the nation's top bed retailers has two weeks of their training program dedicated to how the salesperson should physically position themselves when making a mattress presentation. For example, a male salesman working for this company is always instructed to walk beside the husband and not the wife, as it may trigger subconscious sexual signals.

Kerry Oki was a sales representative employed at a massage parlor. Part of his duties included making cold calls to potential clients in the neighborhood. Anita Coxx was watching a pornographic movie with her insecure husband when the phone rang. Kerri Oki delivered his pitch about the two-for-one massage service and Anita Coxx was picturing a massage with a "happy ending." She could tell that her insecure husband was getting annoyed by hearing her talk to another man on the phone. Anita Coxx knew she had to get out of this call immediately. So she said to Kerri Oki, "Hey, mister, do you want to hear a really cool sound?" Then she slammed the phone down.

"Don't you hate it when someone robs a bank and chooses you to be their hostage?"

—Sidney S. Prasad, Don't Ask Dumb Questions!

Kerry Oki was pissed off after the call. If Anita Coxx were his wife, he'd teach her a lesson for not respecting the humble telemarketer. He'd put birdseeds all over the outside of her car when she was sleeping. That way, when she woke up, there would be a ton of bird shit on there. But he's got to get more creative, since Anita Coxx isn't his wife. Kerri Oki got even by entering Anita Coxx's phone number on a couple of websites that give free automated wake-up calls. Guess who's getting a rude awakening every ten minutes after 3:00 AM Saturday morning?

"Make yourself at home, but keep your hands above the covers."

—Sidney S. Prasad

TELEMARKETER'S REVENGE: THE CUSTOMER IS ALWAYS WRONG, BITCH!

HOARD MY FIST UP YOUR ASS!

If consumers could just be more honest with themselves and in touch with their own inner feelings, then telemarketers would have a much easier job. A lot of prospects play the victimizer role, thinking the world owes them everything on a platter, and then freak out when they realize they aren't going to get it. Rather than taking a breather and asking themselves why they are angry or what they can do to change this situation around, the prospect prefers to bark at everyone in sight and then unload their aggression on the innocent telemarketer who is making a routine sales call.

The smallest things can set people off like a nuclear bomb. For instance, prospect Jack Haas was in front of his fridge one evening, debating whether to feast on sardines and pickles or ketchup and crackers. Jack Haas had a real chip on his shoulder because he was sick of his friends freeloading off his expensive Mr. Noodles and Kraft dinner.

The phone rang, and Jack Haas was anticipating that it would be one of his deadbeat friends calling to share their Thanksgiving pizza. Jack Haas inserted a fork and knife into his pocket as he was reaching for the phone. He was also simultaneously looking for a bib and listening to the caller, who he discovered was a salesman named Dan Singh.

"I didn't call to say that I love you."

—Sidney S. Prasad

Dan Singh was attempting to pitch Jack Haas on storage services. Jack Haas was even more pissed off because he realized he just missed his favorite TV reality show that revolved around hoarding. Jack Haas was in no position to hoard or store anything, because he had only a clock radio, a used mattress that he found in the dump, and a bench that he stole from the park. The bum that originally came with bench was Jack Haas's butler, but he ran away with Jack Haas's blow-up doll.

Even though Jack Haas was at the bottom of the socioeconomic scale, he was a smart cookie, and I'm not talking about a generic brand yellow digestive cookie either. Jack Haas pretended he was hard of hearing and kept interrupting Dan Singh during the presentation, requesting that Dan Singh speak up repeatedly. Then, after a couple of minutes, Jack Haas asked to be transferred to Dan Singh's supervisor. Once the supervisor Don Key came on the line, Jack Haas complained that he was offended that Dan Singh kept screaming at him.

TELEMARKETER'S REVENGE: THE CUSTOMER IS ALWAYS WRONG, BITCH!

Dan Singh was pissed, and normally he would have gone to Jack Haas's car and shoved a couple of bananas up his tailpipe. But Jack Haas's only means of transportation was a bicycle that he leased from his ten-year-old sister.

Dan Singh decided to send Jack Haas a little apology card, with a one-hundred-dollar gift card for a local steakhouse enclosed. That should be enough to cover a decent meal and a few rounds of drinks, right? Wrong! Dan Singh made sure that the card was used and had no money left on it. Dan Singh envisioned Jack Haas washing a pile of dishes and cleaning some crappy toilets with his tongue.

"Oh, hello, Sir! I think we got disconnected, because you forgot to say bye to me!"

—Sidney S. Prasad

SELL OR BE SOLD!

Everything is a sale!

Only a true salesperson can recognize the truth of this statement. Think about when a man approaches a woman in the hope of getting her phone number and asking her out for a date. He essentially is selling himself. If your friend calls you up and states that she has two tickets for the movies and will pick you up at 6:00 PM, then she is pre-closing you and assuming the sale.

The field of selling is one of the most unique industries, as every year, one-third of the people leave the industry, while another one-third enter the field and only one-third remain. All salespeople will agree that what they do takes thick skin. Trust me; getting told to eff off multiple times on a daily basis will definitely thicken the skin of even the weakest people. If you can't handle the heat, then get the fuck out of the kitchen, dipshit!

"My Bipolar Manager is the only guy in the world that gets angry when eating a Happy Meal."

—Sidney S. Prasad, My Bipolar Manager

TELEMARKETER'S REVENGE: THE CUSTOMER IS ALWAYS WRONG, BITCH!

Anna Rexic was a telemarketer with about two years of professional selling experience under her belt. Naturally, when catering to residential clients, the best time to reach a decision-maker is in the evening. One day, around 6:30 PM, Anna Rexic made a cold call to Cole Kutz. Cole Kutz was one of those confused consumers who answer the telephone while having dinner and then bitch about it for the rest of the night.

Anna Rexic started her sales pitch, but was rudely interrupted by Cole Kutz. Cole Kutz asked Anna Rexic if it was her first day, because she sounded pretty shitty. Then, he told her to call back in ten years when she gets her head out of her ass and knows what she is selling. Then the asshole hung up on her.

At this point, some weak salespeople would feel their self-esteem had been beaten on and might even quit their job on the spot, or go home to mama and cry like a little bitch. But who the fuck gives the customer the right to make those snarly comments? Most decent salespeople don't make fun of people when they are at work, whether they are hooking on the street or polishing shoes for a living.

Anna Rexic's gut instincts told her that she should go by Cole Kutz's place and dump a couple of cases of laundry detergent in his swimming pool. But he would just end up cleaning the pool up and it would be over too soon. Since Cole Kutz doesn't like calls during dinner, Anna Rexic put an ad in the local newspaper for a luxury condo for rent at a discounted bargain-basement rate. She also put in Cole Kutz's phone number with special instructions to only call after 6:00 PM.

This should teach him to keep his nasty little comments to himself unless he's looking in the mirror.

"'I'm not interested' is a nice way of saying 'FUCK OFF!'"

—Sidney S. Prasad

TELEMARKETER'S REVENGE: THE CUSTOMER IS ALWAYS WRONG, BITCH!

BROKEN RECORD RULE

Almost every great sales guru will preach that eighty percent of sales are made after the fifth "no." It's common for larger corporations that have call monitoring departments to listen for the sales representative to make five attempts before giving up on the prospect. A lot of weak novice salespeople just give up after the second "no." This is similar to a nagging child or significant other who keeps riding our ass until we give into their petty demands.

Cho Kon It is an ex-telemarketer who is aware of the rule of five "no's." Cho Kon It lasted less than two weeks as a poltergeist-removal salesman, as he claimed there wasn't a market for it. Whenever Cho Kon It is approached by a salesperson, he just shouts "no" five times, and the salesperson gives up.

Dick Mussel was a sales representative promoting timeshares in Harlem and Siberia. Dick Mussel phoned Cho Kon It and attempted to sell him on timeshares. Sure enough, Cho Kon It responded like a broken record with five no's.

"Words can express that you're not interested, but shouting those words out loud can really convey the message."

—Sidney S. Prasad

Dick Mussel isn't no fool and doesn't give up that easy. Dick Mussel continued with his pitch and asking probing questions. This action astonished Cho Kon It, who started answering the probing questions. In the course of the conversation, Cho Kon It revealed that he left the world of telemarketing and became a well-known realtor in their small town. All of a sudden, Cho Kon It turned bipolar or something, as he said "no" five times and hung up.

Dick Mussel pondered making some fake parking tickets and leaving them on Cho Kon It's windshield. But he felt Cho Kon It was too sharp for that, and he needed to kick him in the nuts and kill his market share in the real estate world. Dick Mussel decided to send a transsexual strip-o-gram to Cho Kon It's office. Then, to make the revenge a little sweeter, Dick Mussel put in a bogus report to the business bureau about all the weird sexual activity going on in Cho Kon It's office and how he wasn't sure that it was real estate he was selling.

"I asked My Bipolar Manager how many mood rings he had broken in the last five minutes."

—Sidney S. Prasad, My Bipolar Manager

4 FUCK THE COMPETITION

It blows my mind how television depicts salespeople as lying schmucks. If you ask someone to describe a used car salesman based on what they've seen in the movies and TV, they will likely use the following description: a fast-talking, gold-chain-wearing freak in a plaid suit. Most of the door-to-door salespeople on TV are portrayed as having big teeth and fake smiles pasted across their faces.

I look forward to the day when a TV movie script is written from the salesperson view. I'm talking about rounding up all the salespeople and using their viewpoints to describe the chronic, pathological lying prospect. I guess it's true if you drink enough O.J., you can get away with murder. If I had a nickel for every time a prospect lied to me, I'd be on *Forbes*'s list of the top 100 richest people in the world.

The majority of successful companies in business have a pretty good idea of where their products or services stand in the marketplace. Whether it's offering competitive pricing or additional features and benefits, savvy salespeople know what their competition is offering. The sad reality is that consumers think that salespeople don't do their homework and have no idea that the client is basing their facts on some shit they read out of a fortune cookie.

"Who do you need to consult with before making a decision? Don't you live in a trailer?"

—Sidney S. Prasad

Tim Burr represents a dry-cleaner delivery service and makes cold calls during his downtime. One day, he called up Willie Leak and spoke about the benefits and features of his service. There was only one other competitor in town, and Tim Burr used to work for them. Obviously, Tim Burr was well versed on what the competitor was offering. Willie Leak kept interrupting Tim Burr and made outrageous bogus claims that the competition offered services below cost, along with a bunch of freebies. Tim Burr got sick to his stomach with the bullshit coming out of Willie Leak's mouth and told him that he can't meet or beat the competitor's offering.

Personally, I love the stories when the odd telemarketer loses it with the prospect and confronts them on their bald-faced lies. This sort of behavior is frowned upon, and in most circumstances the telemarketer will receive a serious escalation or even lose their job.

Tim Burr wished he had access to Willie Leak's dry cleaning, as he would put squid and other forms of raw fish in the pockets of his clothes. Life's not that simple, so Tim Burr got even by reporting Willie Leak's car as stolen every day for a week.

TELEMARKETER'S REVENGE: THE CUSTOMER IS ALWAYS WRONG, BITCH!

"I knew this genius asshole who didn't answer the phone when I needed him for a lifeline on *Who Wants To Be A Millionaire*. He told me he was worried that I was a telemarketer."

—Sidney S. Prasad

ONE MAN GANG

Life is really too short to waste on playing games. It's one thing when a prospect keeps telling the salesperson to call them back at another time, and then continually reschedules so both people's time gets wasted. But what's worse is when prospects think they are all cool and fucken' erudite working out a routine to piss off the telemarketer. Why can't consumers just grow some nuts and say that they are not interested?

Inside sales representative Casey Deeya has been selling on the phone for decades and has been exposed to almost every trick in the book. One day, she attempted to solicit Collin Tosayhi, and he pulled a stunt on her that left her breathless. Collin Tosayhi hates telemarketers, but like most consumers wants to make the poor telemarketer's life hell every chance he gets. Collin Tosayhi has a routine worked out with his roommate Curt Tinrod.

"So, let me get this straight; it took you ten minutes to tell me that you don't have time for this?"

—Sidney S. Prasad

Casey Deeya opened with her pitch and Collin Tosayhi listened very carefully to what she was saying and appeared to be very interested in the offer. Every thirty seconds, Curt Tinrod would pick the other phone and say, "Are you done yet, man?" After about the fourth interruption, Casey Deeya was frustrated and asked if Collin Tosayhi if he preferred a callback at a later time when it's convenient. Collin Tosayhi kept responding that it was a convenient time, and he has an hour to kill before work. Curt Tinrod continued to pick up the phone every thirty seconds asking if he was done.

After about the fifteenth interruption in a period of less than ten minutes, Casey Deeya got really angry and ended the call. If she had her way, she would feed hot Tabasco sauce to her Pit bull and let him loose on Collin Tosayhi. But that would be cruelty to animals, so she restrained herself. She looked at Colin Tosayhi's file, made a mock resume, and blasted it to one-thousand-plus companies on the Internet. Now he will have a ringing phone to keep him company when he has time to kill before work. The punishment fit the crime in her book.

TELEMARKETER'S REVENGE: THE CUSTOMER IS ALWAYS WRONG, BITCH!

"Did you want me to get you off or get you off the list?"

—Sidney S. Prasad

SAY, HOW OLD ARE YOU?

Inside salespeople specialize in reading the human voice. They can certainly decipher a buying signal from the prospect, which alerts them to close the sale. On the other hand, inside salespeople can also judge by the client's tone if they need to disclose more information, as the consumer is not 100 percent sold yet. Spending a large portion of the time dealing with prospects on the phone makes it pretty easy to determine if the client is in a genuine rush and it is a bad time. The client's tone can also reveal that they are receptive to listening to the sales speech.

Horace Cope specialized in the sale of residential and commercial fences. He made a cold call to Hayden Seek. Horace Cope started pitching discounted residential fencing to Hayden Seek. Hayden Seek was offended by the product, as he lived in an apartment and didn't have a fence to worry about. He sort of felt like it was a random call from a list and he wasn't an eligible prospect.

Consumers fail to understand that sometimes a phone number on a calling list was once upon a time a qualified lead. If the person moves or changes phone numbers, the telemarketers are the last ones to know this vital piece of information until it's brought to their attention.

"I don't drink, smoke or gamble but I'm a fucken' chronic, pathological liar!"

—Sidney S. Prasad, My Bipolar Manager

Like most smart consumers, Hayden Seek decided to show his true asshole colors. He said he was fourteen years old and that it was illegal for him to be having this conversation with Horace Cope. After dealing with thousands of different unique voices on the phone, it's not hard to determine if there's a minor or an adult speaking. It was obvious by Hayden Seek's voice that he was at least fifty years old, or older with his dried-up smoker's cough. Horace Cope requested to speak to Hayden's father and Hayden Seek responded, "I'm a bastard," and hung up the phone.

Horace Cope wasn't a dummy and he knew what was going on. Horace Cope felt like rubbing Krazy Glue all over Hayden Seek's toilet seat, but that would be letting him off too easy. Horace Cope knew that apartment buildings had really tiny mailboxes and sometimes the overfull mail gets hand delivered by the landlord. So he mailed him over twenty raunchy pornographic movies and a dozen dirty magazines. Maybe after watching a couple of movies, he can learn to make some bastard children of his own.

TELEMARKETER'S REVENGE: THE CUSTOMER IS ALWAYS WRONG, BITCH!

"Roses are red, violets are blue, I couldn't finish the rest of this poem because a fucken' telemarketer kept interrupting my thoughts of you."

—Sidney S. Prasad

BEING AN ASSHOLE IS FUN

I guess it's sort of a double-edged sword; most decent telemarketers will remove a prospect's phone number after a formal request has been made. However, there are those rare exceptions where we actually get a kick out of listening to the nut on the other line go psycho on us so we have something to talk about at lunchtime. If a customer wants to get pissy, then why not send the love back and piss in their cornflakes?

Max E. Padd was a part-time telemarketer while studying to become a gynecologist. He really didn't give a crap if he lost his job tomorrow, as one day he'd be making the big bucks inspecting pee-pees. There was this one customer in the database named Wilma Dickfit who was like the biggest cow on the planet. She requested to be removed from the calling list several times. However, she went about it the wrong way, demeaning the poor telemarketers. Naturally, they kept her name and number in the database and kept rescheduling her for callbacks by various agents.

"Breaking up with a telemarketer is the hardest thing to do. Because they will call back five times to ask you why you aren't interested."

—Sidney S. Prasad

Wilma Dickfit thought she would fight back and make the telemarketing firm take her number off the residential calling list. She knew that those little shits would call her every night around 6:30 PM. Like clockwork, one night the phone rang. She recognized the number, so she answered like this: "Good evening, Anita Dyck's Sex Line, all calls are $2.99 per minute, starting now."

The telemarketer, Ivan Odor, was caught off guard and chuckled, then hung up the phone. Ivan Odor was about to remove the number off their list and then realized it was Wilma Dickfit's house. Who could forget a name like Wilma Dickfit, right? Ivan Odor wished he had a picture of Wilma Dickfit so he could post it on THEDIRTY.COM and make some rumors that she's bad in bed.

Ivan Odor got creative and called up a Tupperware agent, then a sex toy party agent, and a couple more agents and scheduled some in-home demonstrations for Wilma Dickfit.

TELEMARKETER'S REVENGE: THE CUSTOMER IS ALWAYS WRONG, BITCH!

"Let me put on speakerphone so my whole family can tell you to fuck off!"

—Sidney S. Prasad

OH, BEHAVE!

Have you ever heard people talk about the glory days of pagers? When your pager beeped, you could decide if you wanted to invest a quarter and call the person back. This came in handy for those people that you were purposely avoiding because it was your turn to buy the beer. A lot of people claimed they got a lot more done when pagers were around and had a lot more control over their lives. Well, cell phones and most house phones aren't different, as most phones in both categories are equipped with a ring silencer and a call display.

What I'm trying to say is if someone is trying to milk a cow or breastfeed a baby or rub their bare ass on their mother-in-law's dentures, then why not turn the phone off? You could definitely concentrate a lot easier, especially if the dentures had a gold tooth in them, as you might get your bum hair caught in it. Ella Funt had spent the last hour trying to put her little shit to sleep. Finally, the baby fell asleep, and Ella Funt was looking forward to going outside and smoking a funny cigarette with her neighbor. As she started tippy-toeing out of the room, the phone rang.

"Freedom of speech doesn't give you the right to call me first thing in the morning and pitch credit card insurance."

—Sidney S. Prasad

Inside sales representative Gabe Oy was on the other end with the deal of the century for her. Ella Funt was choked up because the baby started crying and pissing once his call awakened her. There wasn't a moment of silence, so Ella Funt put the crying little shit next to the phone. Eventually Gabe Oy hung up, as he would rather get each one of his pubic hairs pulled out simultaneously than listen to a crying baby.

Gabe Oy would love to get into Ella Funt's kitchen and make her some fresh urine popsicles, but she probably liked that freaky shit. Gabe Oy wanted Ella Funt to cry like a miserable shit when she woke up to get even. After work, Gabe Oy and his telemarketing buddies went to Ella Funt's driveway and drew a chalk line of someone's body. They also left a couple of empty bullet shells close by and smeared some ketchup on the driveway. They were pretty sure this would make her shit herself crying.

"Telemarketing is a tough racket. Either you sell the client or they sold you!"

—Sidney S. Prasad

5 POOPER SCOOPER

Technology is advancing at an alarming rate, and at the same time, people are becoming even lazier to complement that. Over a century ago, people had to depend on the horse and carriage to get themselves around. There were no blenders or food processors to dice their vegetables, as that was all done by hand. Society today is totally taking advantage of the benefits of technology. Fuck, no one wants to even walk, as so many airports have those moving sidewalks and the people who aren't flying are using those ugly portable scooters. Rather than use free time wisely to work out and be more physical, Man chooses to park his fat ass in front of the television, shoveling processed junk food in his mouth, while texting the fast food restaurants to bring him some more shit to eat. People have no time to think about the ozone layer crisis because they are too busy increasing their waistline bigger than the equator.

Consumers tend to complain about the strangest shit that salespeople proposition them with. What the consumer fails to realize is that the average sane company isn't going to invest millions of dollars into a product or service and get their sales force to push it if there weren't a market for it. Believe it or not, there is a large market that caters to consumers who refuse to wash their shit-stained soiled underwear. This type of consumer enjoys the comfort of sitting in their poop-filled adult diapers while playing video games. As salespeople, we have to scope out the marketplace and locate these degenerates and sell them their shit.

"I picked up this chick at the bar last night and we exchanged phone numbers. I called her the next day and pitched her on switching long distance carriers. She seemed kind of surprised at first. I told her she should have asked me what I do for a living when she gave me her number."

—Sidney S. Prasad

Harry Cox was hosting a wild, off-the-wall party. He invited all of his buddies from band camp, chess club, and the library committee. The party was really happening with a Monopoly tournament on one end of the room and dominos on the other side. Everybody was enjoying the Kool Aid that Harry Cox's mom had made.

Telemarketer Doris Clitoris phoned up Harry Cox and pitched him on some doggy-doo-doo removal services. Harry Cox was pissed off because he was just about to hit on a foreign exchange student from ESL class named Hoo Flung Poo. Harry Cox was enraged, so he accused Doris Clitoris of running a conspiracy scam. He confidently said that Doris Clitoris's company was purposely shitting on people's lawn at night and then offering to pick up the shit the next day for a premium price. Harry Cox then raised his voice, threatened to call the cops and start a shit storm, then hung up.

TELEMARKETER'S REVENGE: THE CUSTOMER IS ALWAYS WRONG, BITCH!

This was a case where the consumer neglected to realize how fucken' lazy his fellow species is and there was indeed a market for picking up dog shit. Doris Clitoris didn't appreciate the way she was treated by Harry Cox. She thought in her head that if she had a right mind, she'd take a shit on his air conditioner vents. But she knew she needed to conserve her shit just in case she had to crap on a prospect's lawn to increase her market share.

After work, she snuck onto Harry Cox's property and killed his lawn, pouring a combination of ammonia, bleach, and gasoline on it. Harry Cox is going to wish only he had dog shit on his lawn.

"The best way to break up with a gold-digger is tell her that you are on welfare."

—Sidney S. Prasad, Plenty Of Freaks: Are You Sold On Online Dating?

SIDNEY S. PRASAD

FAMILY TREE–HUGGER

Consumers act all high-and-fucken'-mighty when they are hiding behind their phone lines. Door-to-door salesmen don't get abused as badly as telemarketers do. It's quite amusing how lonely nerdy consumers all of a sudden grow nuts overnight. They feel all strong and mighty when they're sitting with their trailer trash family and friends sharing a bucket of chicken and homemade beer.

Iman S. Hole had the privilege of soliciting long distance plans to almost any potential residential client nationwide. He decided to call up some rednecks in the middle of some boonie town in Texas. Denton Fender answered the phone and empathetically listened to Iman S. Hole's pitch. He then instructed him to hold on while he grabbed his gay lover, who is the man of the house. The phone then got passed around and five different male voices told Iman S. Hole to go fuck himself and all the people in his family tree.

Iman S. Hole wished that he could get on a plane, sneak into Denton Fender's medicine cabinet, and poke pinholes in his condoms. This was just wishful thinking, as it would be a fantasy to have access to a private jet to get even with all the assholes that ever pissed him off. Thanks to the help of social media websites, Iman S. Hole was able to get the name and phone number of Denton Fender's workplace. Then, he got his sweet revenge by getting all of his telemarketing colleagues to make bogus harassing collection calls at his work.

TELEMARKETER'S REVENGE: THE CUSTOMER IS ALWAYS WRONG, BITCH!

"Answering the telephone without looking at the call display is sort of like a blind man picking a porno."

—Sidney S. Prasad

TREAT THEM LIKE DOGS

Consumers purchase products that cater to their lifestyles for several reasons. There could be one lard-ass whose goal is to have every restaurant in the Yellow Pages deliver food to him. This is probably because he doesn't have enough butter at his place to grease his ass out the door and put a couple of buffets out of business. Then, there are those special-occasion clients who work their tails off and splurge once in a blue moon and purchase some Girl Guide cookies. Lastly, we are left with people who could genuinely benefit from the actual service. For example, if someone has health restrictions or are elderly, they could recognize the value of paying someone to shovel their snow. It's a win-win situation.

"People who choose to live in glass houses shouldn't watch porn on big screen televisions."

—Sidney S. Prasad, People Who Choose To Live in Glass Houses

Bea Apal was employed at an animal lovers' enterprise. The company specialized in pet grooming, pet day care, and dog-walking. She made a cold call to Sid Downe and offered professional dog-walking services. Sid Downe was in a consumer category that we forgot about, which is the type of consumer who would love to purchase anything presented to them, but never has enough funds to cover it on their two-figure sandwich-artist salary.

Sid Downe decided to be cocky. He was willing to purchase Bea Apal's services under one condition: he required Bea Apal to provide a criminal record clearance document indicating Bea Apal had no bestiality charges. Bea Apal did both of them a favor and hung up the phone.

Bea Apal fantasized about Sid Downe working in the same facility as her. She would wait for the day Sid Downe was in the shitter, reading the funnies, and pull the fire alarm on his stinky ass. Bea Apal's recipe for revenge involved using a tape recorder to record the echoes of a dog screaming as it was getting its nails clipped. She then phoned the SPCA from a payphone and identified herself as Sid Downe's next door neighbor. She explained that Sid Downe constantly abused his dog and played the tape recorder into the phone.

TELEMARKETER'S REVENGE: THE CUSTOMER IS ALWAYS WRONG, BITCH!

"Telemarketers are perverted because they always call me when I'm having sex."

—Sidney S. Prasad

WHO'S THE ADULT?

There's a time and place when one should act childish. Like if you take your kids to an amusement park, or you're hosting a five-year-old's birthday party and want to fit in with the kids. But it's scary when you see a grown man cry like a little bitch. Or when you hear some forty-five-year-old cougar talking like a kid when the waiter brings the dessert over.

Ray Pist was employed as a sales representative for an Internet provider. Naturally, he was mandated to call up people in the community and promote discount Internet subscriptions. I'm an advocate of getting as many residential clients hooked up to the Internet as possible, because it makes life easier. If more people had the Internet at home, then we wouldn't have to worry about those boneheads that watch porn on library computers and touch themselves in public.

"Don't change your sexual orientation for me, but I wouldn't mind if you switched your Internet providers though."

—Sidney S. Prasad

Ray Pist contacted Stan Backk to see if he would be interested in a complimentary Internet trial. Stan Backk was kind of peeved and paranoid because he was in the middle of ripping off some money from his kid's piggy bank to pay the pizza man with. Rather than accepting or declining Ray Pist's offer, Stan Backk kept repeating everything Ray Pist said until Ray Pist hung up.

Ray Pist felt like sticking some poison ivy in Stan Backk's pool and make his balls swell for the way he behaved. Ray Pist thought about it for a moment and thought he could give him a dirtier burn. Ray Pist created an online dating profile and pretended to be a twenty-one-year-old busty blonde. He then started chatting with a dude named Dane Jeriss. Ray Pist told him that "her" parents were gone on vacation and to come over with a bottle of wine and a box of condoms at the stroke of midnight. (Keep in mind that Ray Pist gave Stan Backk's address to Dan Jeriss.)

Later that night Ray Pist and his boiler-room buddies parked close to Stan's home. They got entertained by watching Dane Jeriss and Stan Backk getting into a scrap.

"Why can't telemarketers use their brains and call during TV commercials?"

—Sidney S. Prasad

6 BRAINIAC PARENTS VS. DUMB KIDS

It's funny how a lot of Baby Boomers say children are a lot dumber today compared to their generation. It's a yes-and-no statement. I do believe the Baby Boomer generation was forced to use their brains a little bit more than the new generation is. For instance, thirty years ago, all of those complicated math problems were figured out on paper, while today it's just a couple of key strokes on a calculator. People today definitely rely and lean on technology a lot more than yesterday's generation.

As a career salesman, I strongly believe the onus is on the parent in the event their dumb kid pulls them out of the shower to answer a sales call. The parent shouldn't shit all over the telemarketer, right? It's a negative reflection on the parents' end that they never taught the ABC's of answering the phone, screening calls, and taking messages.

One day, Carl Arm phoned Manny Kin's home. Her child answered the phone and said to hold on, as her mom was outside.

"You tell your kids not to talk to strangers, yet you let them answer the telephone."

—Sidney S. Prasad

Manny Kin was a cheap shit and didn't want to buy her produce from a grocery store. She was in the garden, using dog shit as fertilizer to grow some carrots. Carl Arm overheard the child telling her mom that he was a man trying to sell discounted 1979 encyclopedias on the phone. Carl Arm could understand that Manny Kin was frustrated that her daughter went out of her way to interrupt her gardening. A simple "I'm not interested" would have done the trick. Instead, Manny Kin bumped her car, set the alarm off, and then placed the phone beside it to piss off the salesman.

Carl Arm would love to put some roadkill on Manny Kin's barbecue to help her save money on her butcher's bill. But why not give this bitch a taste of her own medicine, he thought? So, that night, between the hours of 11:00 PM and 4:30 AM, Carl Arm would sneak by and set off Manny Kin's car alarm every twenty minutes.

"Teach a man to fish and you fed him for the day. Teach a man to ruin someone's seafood dinner and you got a telemarketer."

—Sidney S. Prasad

TELEMARKETER'S REVENGE: THE CUSTOMER IS ALWAYS WRONG, BITCH!

DON'T BUY IT!

The beauty of being a telemarketer is you can develop your skills to an expert level in a short time. What am I referring to, in terms of expertise? Well, when you are calling on fifty to two hundred clients per day, pitching the exact same product or service, then you pretty much have a good idea when the prospects are lukewarm or ice cold. Responses like, "let me sleep on it," translate to "I'm letting you off the hook today because I'm in a good mood and don't feel like telling you to go fuck your mother." Or when a prospect tells you to send something in the mail, that's a nice way of saying, "Fuck off." When a client keeps rescheduling callbacks, they are signaling the telemarketer to give up, because they are too chicken-shit to tell them that they are not interested.

As sales pros, we expect to hear a certain amount of "no," "fuck off," "get me off your list," and "I'll take it!" before we even start our shifts. It's those creative and innovative little bastards that sometimes catch us off guard and cheese us right off.

It was Friday night and Gene E. Us just got paid his two-figure paycheck. Unfortunately, after paying off an indecent exposure fine, the bulk of his paycheck was spoken for. Gene E. Us was feeling quite hungry and wandered into his roommate's room. He rummaged through her underwear drawers, checking for loose change.

SIDNEY S. PRASAD

"Don't lie; just say you don't want to buy."

—Sidney S. Prasad

Gene E. Us was on a roll. He was about to break the two-dollar mark and could picture himself dining with the rich and famous at McDonald's that night. All of a sudden, the phone rang; it was Faye Slift on the other end, pitching him on a home renovation package.

Gene E. Us was normally an asshole when it came to dealing with telemarketers. However, he had bigger fish to fry, and just wanted to end the call politely. His response to Faye Slift's pitch was, "Oh my God, we work in the same company. But, sorry. According to the employee handbook, we are restricted from soliciting to our coworkers. Thank you for thinking of me with your call." He then hung up the telephone.

Faye Slift felt totally bamboozled and knew that Gene E. Us didn't work with her, because there were less than half a dozen people employed by that family-owned company. With the exception of Faye Slift, everyone at her workplace had the same middle name, Harry, and the last name Beaver. Faye Slift wished that she had access to a couple of fake licenses with Gene E. Us's information on it, because she would do a couple of eat-and-runs and leave the licenses on the seat.

TELEMARKETER'S REVENGE: THE CUSTOMER IS ALWAYS WRONG, BITCH!

According to the information in Faye Slift's database, Gene E. Us was a bachelor, so Faye Slift decided to help him get married. She thought she would do him a favor and get him out of his misery of loneliness and order him a mail-order bride.

"Can you imagine someone calling you at work and hanging up on you every two minutes for an eight hour shift? Can you imagine that happening for the duration of your career? Then I guess you know what it feels like to be a telemarketer."

—Sidney S. Prasad

THE PRICE IS WRONG, BITCH!

Whether you are the richest man in the world, or a poor starving child in a third-world country, or somewhere in the middle like you and I, the one thing that makes us equal is that God doesn't discriminate and gives us all the same twenty four hours in a day and seven days per week.

The scary thing is how much time the average person wastes. One study revealed that the average person watches five hours of TV per day. When you do the math, that translates to losing almost three months per year. If you waste five minutes each day, that means you've lost over one full calendar day out of your year. That's some scary shit, eh?

Salespeople can appreciate that the customer's time is just as valuable as the salesperson's time. But what we can't fathom is why customers freak out when we interrupt them at home. Like the customer was secretly working on a nuclear warhead in their basement when we called. Or maybe they were digging an underground railroad and decided to answer the ringing phone.

TELEMARKETER'S REVENGE: THE CUSTOMER IS ALWAYS WRONG, BITCH!

Doris Ajar was a mid-level interior decorator who catered to the middle class. Howie Dewitt was moving up in the world, as he just moved out of the projects and got a great deal on a trailer home because the occupants died in it last summer when their air conditioner gave out in the middle of the night. Howie Dewitt was an environmentalist and cared very deeply about Mother Nature. He wanted to save a couple of trees and refused to receive a cable bill in the mail. So, after his neighbor left for the evening to hijack a hotdog cart, Howie Dewitt spent the night illegally fishing his neighbor's cable over to his trailer.

"Sorry I answered the phone; I thought it was someone important."

—Sidney S. Prasad

Later, Howie Dewitt had decided to take a break and try on some of his wife's dresses when the phone started ringing. Doris Ajar's European accent was too classy for Howie Dewitt, and he had no need for her interior decorating services because his décor consisted of some traffic signs and some stolen finger paintings. Rather than being completely honest with Doris Ajar and just telling her that he wasn't a suitable client, Howie Dewitt stuck the phone in the microwave and closed the door. He did this so Doris Ajar could hear how ridiculous she sounded complemented by the echoes of the microwave.

Doris Ajar was aggravated and felt insulted, but she did feel that she sounded pretty sexy on the phone. If Howie Dewitt were Doris Ajar's husband, she would shave off his eyebrows in the middle of the night or put laxatives in his food. She thought of a better way to get even with our friend, Mr. Environmental. She announced to a couple of charities that Howie Dewitt was going to donate his trailer, car, and all his possessions to them. Howie Dewitt wouldn't know what hit him when all the charities came knocking on his door to collect.

"My phone number is reserved for close family, friends, and important business affiliates, and you don't fit either category."

—Sidney S. Prasad

TELEMARKETER'S REVENGE: THE CUSTOMER IS ALWAYS WRONG, BITCH!

WAKE ME UP BEFORE YOU GO GO

Hotels can be accommodating, especially when they are clean with no bedbugs and have no love stains on the sheets. The beauty of hotels is the futuristic technology they use to help their patrons sleep. The technology that I'm referring to is that each room comes with a "Do Not Disturb" sign. Someone interested in having a nice comfy rest just pops that sign on the door and the cleaning staff will get the hint and fuck off.

Life would be easier for both customer and telemarketer if there was a "do not disturb" signal on the telephone. The obvious thing is to turn your ringer off when you don't want to be disturbed or just throw your phone into the backyard for a couple of hours, as it will give your dog a nice little toy to slobber on for the evening.

Homer Run has been working his tail off at his part-time job at the tollbooth. He felt his hands were getting tired from collecting money for four hours per day while he sat on his fat rump. Homer Run thought he would treat himself to a sick day and catch up on his beauty sleep. (Trust me; if you'd ever seen this guy, you would tell him to take a beauty hibernation for at least six months.)

"You can delete a spam message because it's not human but swearing at a telemarketer is inhumane."

—Sidney S. Prasad

Brighton Early was a telemarketer who randomly came across Homer Run's phone number and called him up, which woke up Homer Run. Homer Run was choked up, but wasn't sure if he was mad at Brighton Early for waking him up or the goldfish bowl cleaning service that he was trying to sell him on. Brighton Early works for one of those stupid firms that give all the power to the customers; if a client asks you to scratch their nuts or shave their back, you're pretty much stuck doing it.

Homer Run requested that Brighton Early do a Google search for the "Do-Not-Call Registry." Once Brighton Early gave him that number, Homer Run said to call him in ten minutes and enjoy the fine.

From a telemarketer's point of view, that was a pretty dick move of Homer Run to do. Personally, no job is worth that kind of harassment. If I were the telemarketer on the line, I'd be tempted to call the power company and shut off his electricity to put this loser in his place. If I had his email address, I'd be tempted to send him naked pictures of senior citizens and obese people.

TELEMARKETER'S REVENGE: THE CUSTOMER IS ALWAYS WRONG, BITCH!

Brighton Early had a sadistic side to him, as well. Later that night, Brighton Early, accompanied by his telemarketing crew, borrowed a CPR dummy from their employer. Then they stuck it halfway underneath Homer Run's car, so all you could see was the legs sticking out. They also got a couple bottles of ketchup and spread it underneath the CPR dummy's body.

"Reverse psychology is for suckers. I told a telemarketer that I'm not interested, and he called the next five nights straight!"

—Sidney S. Prasad

7 DUMB ASS!

At the end of the day, regardless of color, sex, ethnicity, or sexual orientation, we are all human and we all bleed and shit the same way. It sometimes surprises people in the customer service field how nasty and cruel prospects can get. Some fucken' customers think the world is over because a telemarketer interrupted them during a rerun of *Seinfeld* that they were watching for the fifth time. Here's a thought: Why not just buy the whole series so you can watch it anytime? Or if we call a prospect during dinnertime, they act like we interrupted them while having a seven course meal with the Queen of England, when in reality they were fighting over the last few noodles of canned spaghetti. I wish I could tell these losers to get some class and defrost a TV dinner.

Ivana Tinkle was an All-American girl who still lived with her parents while in her forties. She borrowed her dad's Cadillac the other night for a special night with her boyfriend. He just got parole and they had to make up for lost time. She was busy cleaning the love stains off the back seat with her father's toothbrush when the phone rang. Frank N. Beans was calling to offer her a discounted pornographic cable package. She thought about it for a second, but she knew she wasn't really into the visuals of porn. Plus, she was okay listening to her eighty-year-old parents go at it every night through the heat vents for free.

TELEMARKETER'S REVENGE: THE CUSTOMER IS ALWAYS WRONG, BITCH!

"Hollywood claims that the camera adds ten pounds. What is your excuse?"

—Sidney S. Prasad, Plenty OF Freaks: Are You Sold On Online Dating?

Like most typical customers when telemarketers call, she had to be a little bitch about it. She asked Frank N. Beans the following question: "If you were me, would you purchase this service?" Frank N. Beans paused and said, "Hell, yeah, I would buy it, and also add in the roadkill cooking channel too!" Ivana Tinkle responded, "Well, you're *not* me," and hung up the telephone.

Frank N. Beans drove by Ivana Tinkle's home that night and started laying down a spike belt under her father's car. But his conscience caught up with him and he couldn't do it. As an alternative, he called up a bookie and placed some gigantic bets with outrageously unfavorable odds on behalf of Ivana Tinkle.

"Everything in life is a sale, and you still haven't sold me on why you are not interested, Sir."

—Sidney S. Prasad

PENNY PINCHERS

The economic history of the last decade has been incredible. So many Internet millionaires were made overnight just by investing a few bucks in some bow-wow company. Then the real estate market took off like a rocket, and everyone and their dog were flipping homes like soiled underwear. I remember reading an article a few years back stating that during the peak of the real estate boom, one in seventy California residents had a real estate license. That just blew me away, considering that the state of California's population was equivalent to the entire population of Canada.

During the real estate boom, it wasn't unusual for a realtor to knock on someone's door and offer to sell their home. Cold calls from realtors were also a part of the daily telemarketing calls prospects would receive.

There are certain times of the day when salespeople don't mind being told to fuck off or hung up on. This includes five minutes prior to our coffee break or lunch break. Right around 11:45 AM, telemarketers are preoccupied thinking about their reservations at some expensive upscale restaurant in the mall food court.

TELEMARKETER'S REVENGE: THE CUSTOMER IS ALWAYS WRONG, BITCH!

"To kill multiple people makes one a serial killer. To ruin multiple people's dinner makes one a telemarketer."

—Sidney S. Prasad

Hope Todye was a lead generator and was paid at an hourly rate. Her mandate was to call residential prospects and probe if they were interesting in listing their homes. She was instructed to pass the phone to the realtor when she came across the odd sucker interested in selling their home in the upscale part of Harlem.

It was about two minutes to Hope Todye's break and she was looking forward to a quick customer hang-up when she called up Herb Avore. Herb Avore was a fucken' geek who had no life. He was the kind of guy who took his sister as a prom date. His attire was complemented by a pocket protector and clip-on calculator. The sad thing was that he sort of welcomed telemarketing calls because he adored the company, but would never buy. Herb Avore's goal was to keep the telemarketer on the phone as long as possible. This would allow him to brag to his buddies in chess club that he was on the phone all night with someone with a sexy voice (regardless of their sex).

"Smoking cigarettes, drinking alcohol, and hanging up on telemarketers are addictive."

—Sidney S. Prasad

Hope Todye enquired if whether Herb Avore was interested in listing his home. Herb Avore said, "No, but I'm actually thinking of purchasing a second home. Hold on while I grab my piggy bank." Let's just say Hope Todye spent the next three hours listening to Herb Avore count his change. Every time, right when Hope Todye was about to fall asleep, Herb Avore would yell out, "Yay, a nickel!" The call resulted in Herb Avore not being qualified to purchase a second home, because he only had $120 in loose change.

Hope Todye was fuming and she combed through the Internet looking for bumper stickers for Herb Avore's car that said, "I SUPPORT TERRORISM." But unfortunately she couldn't track any down. She thought, why not take a chance and break into Herb Avore's house? At the worst, if she got caught, Herb Avore would probably make her stay and play board games with him all night.

So Hope Todye snuck into Herb Avore's home around 7:30 PM, when he was fast asleep with his thumb in his mouth. Then, Hope Todye got busy and hid a dozen alarm clocks at various spots in Herb Avore's home. Hope Todye wanted Herb Avore to get the message and learn the definition of time as those hidden clocks went off periodically throughout the night.

TELEMARKETER'S REVENGE: THE CUSTOMER IS ALWAYS WRONG, BITCH!

"A good salesman can sell the shirt off his back; a great salesman can sell his clothes to a nudist camp."

—Sidney S. Prasad

LET'S BE HONEST

Since childhood, people all over the world have been taught that honesty is the best policy…unless you work for the government. A person can formulate an impression within the first thirty seconds of meeting someone. I truly believe that if a person can't respond within the first twenty seconds of being asked a question, then it's not a true answer their lips are delivering. I'm not one for taking the phone into the shitter, but the odd time that my pants are down and I answer my cell phone, I'll be honest with the caller. I have no hesitation in telling my editor, girlfriend, or the credit card company that I'm taking a big, fat, juicy, mango-sized shit. They usually let me finish my shit in peace and allow me to call them back.

A lot of telemarketers are bothered by the games that prospects play because they accidentally picked up the phone. It's not the telemarketers' fault that the client finds it too stressfully challenging to balance a TV remote control in one hand and the telephone in the other. If a prospect told a telemarketer that they were expecting an important call and it's not the right time, the telemarketer would gladly excuse the prospect. But consumers, for some reason, find it easier to play games and insult he telemarketers rather than be honest.

TELEMARKETER'S REVENGE: THE CUSTOMER IS ALWAYS WRONG, BITCH!

"Don't you hate it when your blind date ends up being your ex-husband?"

—Sidney S. Prasad, Don't Ask Dumb Questions!

Joe Mama was busy trimming his pubic hairs with his roommate's nose-tweezers when the phone rang. Telemarketer Leo Tarred could tell by the tone of Joe Mama's voice that he was doing something important. But Leo Tarred knew his boss was periodically tuning into his phone calls and he would get in major shit if he told the prospect that they sounded busy and he would call back. Leo Tarred went on with his pitch, promoting trash-removal services.

Joe Mama knew right away that he wasn't a qualified prospect because he hardly accumulated garbage. He worked for minimum wage as the bouncer of a wholesale club, and therefore can't afford to buy jack shit. He pretty much lived off free samples and the food that he stole from the birds in the park. The odd time that he had trash, he just dumped it on his boss's lawn. Joe Mama could have just been honest and shared his situation with Leo Tarred and everything would be hunky dory. However, Joe Mama decided to say "your mama" after every second word Leo Tarred said until he hung up on him.

Leo Tarred imagined sticking Joe Mama's face in the toilet and then using his face as human toilet paper. But he knew he had to do something profound that would make him laugh for the next couple of weeks. Leo Tarred took Joe Mama's information with him to the post office during his lunch break. He then did an immediate change-of-address to a country that he couldn't pronounce on the other side of the planet. Pretty sweet revenge for a salesman that specializes in taking junk out of your trunk!

"I love it when people tell me that they don't speak English. Especially when their television has the evening news blaring in the background."

—Sidney S. Prasad

TELEMARKETER'S REVENGE: THE CUSTOMER IS ALWAYS WRONG, BITCH!

CHOKE ON IT

I've heard of people being so dumb that they would believe practically anything that someone told them, such as:

1) Believing that it wasn't their boyfriend kissing their best friend, but his twin brother.
2) The guy with the jalopy clunker convincing his date that his Porsche was in the shop and the shitty car was his courtesy car.
3) The woman with aftershave, men's razor blades, and guy clothes in her apartment claiming that they belong to her brother who is a trucker that occasionally stops by.
4) Someone who pours generic pop into a Coke bottle and attempts to convince you that it's real Coke.
5) Teenagers that convince their parents that the library is open 24/7 so they can sneak into nightclubs with their fake IDs.

There's a fine line between being really stupid and extremely gullible. But the best way to bust a chronic pathological liar is to ask them the same question on different occasions and watch their house of cards tumble.

"Why are you asking me, 'who's there?' This isn't a fucken' knock-knock joke!"

—Sidney S. Prasad

Eden Run was a telemarketer who promoted a mobile adult-diaper disposal service. One day, she called up Yaura Stinker to see if this service intrigued him. Yaura Stinker apparently was a Class-A bullshit artist and a quick thinker, which go hand-in-hand with each other. Yaura Stinker carefully listened to Eden Run's pitch and responded that he was a squatter and not sure when the homeowners were coming back home.

There is a classic funny scenario where someone is robbing or squatting in a home and decides to answer the phone and talk to a telemarketer. The salesperson would have to be extremely mentally challenged to believe this crock of shit. If Yaura Stinker was actually telling the truth and was a squatter, then I'd personally hire the biggest, meanest-looking guard dog to sit and man the door and not let the creep out till the rightful owners returned home. But it's not me in this scenario, and Eden Run had a pretty clever idea of her own.

With the assistance of a scanner and laser-printer technology, she doctored a pizza flyer and stuck Yaura Stinker's phone number on it. Then, she made about five hundred copies and had them sent out all over town. Let's see how long Yaura Stinker can continue using the same lame-ass excuse of being a squatter.

"It's hard to believe that you accidentally answered the phone while sitting on the shitter. However, it's quite easy to believe that you forgot to wash your hands."

—Sidney S. Prasad

8 CRYING WOLF

Whether selling on the phone, in a showroom, or peddling door-to-door, one will encounter all walks of life and all levels of sanity. Salespeople are accustomed to people lying to their face, swearing profanities in their ears, and chasing them out of their offices. Thick skin is at the foundation of any successful salesperson, as they can tolerate almost any situation presented to them in life.

Occasionally, though, there will be the odd prospect that can surprise even the most advanced veteran salesperson. I'm talking about the time when telemarketer Burton Ernie called Wong Tern.

Burton Ernie was employed at a college-based painting company and arranged residential appointments for his team to paint. One day, he decided to call upon Wong Tern, who I guess was in the middle of vacuuming the lint out of his belly button when the phone rang. After listening to Burton Ernie's sales pitch, the image of some young hoodlums rummaging through his wife panty drawer while getting drunk on his beer dashed through Wong Tern's mind. "If anyone is going to touch my wife's sticky, second-hand panties, it's going to be me," Wong Tern thought. So, rather than just saying plain-out "no" or hanging up, Wong Tern purposely started crying like a little bitch for a few minutes and wouldn't stop until Burton Ernie hung up.

"One who is at bliss with the creator will come across crazy to an insane man. However, one who is in denial of the creator will appear insane to the spiritual man!"

—Sidney S. Prasad, My Bipolar Manager

Burton Ernie was blown away by the tremendously well-done burn from Wong Tern. Burton Ernie fantasized about Wong Tern going to the same college as him, because then he would mix up some fake cocaine using sugar and flour, plant it in Wong Tern's locker, and call Campus Security. Burton Ernie remembered that Wong Tern had a thick foreign accent, and knew just the remedy in getting even with this crying bastard. Burton Ernie called up immigration, made a phony illegal alien complaint, and gave Wong Tern's name, number, and address. Now let Wong Tern cry his way out of this one while getting loaded onto a boat like human cargo.

"When you meet someone virtually and the date is going sour, too bad you can't hit delete or throw them in the recycle bin."

—Sidney S. Prasad, Plenty Of Freaks: Are You Sold On Online Dating?

CAN'T CONTAIN MYSELF

We are all guilty of giving or receiving gifts that the other person had no use for. Like, it's pointless giving underwear and socks to someone who prefers to roll commando in sandals, right? Or giving beer to a wine drinker or *vice versa*. If you want to piss off a vegetarian, keep offering them meat or give them a gift card for a steakhouse.

There are certain products out on the marketplace that some consumers can't picture anyone using. If your husband's a fat beer-guzzling slob who hasn't seen his penis since Bill Clinton was in office and you sleep in separate rooms, then I can conclude that you would have no use for birth control. Besides, he'd probably mistake those pills for Tic-Tacs and eat them, too.

However, there are certain products that you don't use on a daily basis, but once in a blue moon, when the occasion arises, you are so happy that you own it or have coverage. A lot of people who live in small redneck towns prefer to communicate only with the hicks they grew up with, wrestling cattle together and having cockfights. But on that odd occasion when they need to get a hold of their Uncle Elmer who's doing time in an out-of-state prison for bestiality offenses, it's great to have a long-distance carrier.

"Relax. I'm not trying to sell you on religion, but I am trying to persuade you into subscribing to the Sunday paper."

—Sidney S. Prasad

Al Beback was a deadbeat who would cash his welfare checks at the liquor store and go to the sperm bank just before a ritzy date at Burger King. One day, while Al Beback's roommate was fast asleep, he was busy licking the cream off her Oreo cookies. He was in the midst of planting the bag of cookies by his roommate's dog when the phone rang. Bruce Easily was on the other end of the line, trying to convince him to purchase accidental insurance. Al Beback decided to be a smart-ass and responded, "Speaking of accidents, I just shit myself," and hung up on Bruce Easily.

Bruce Easily decided to piss this fool off and max out his credit on pornography website memberships. The problem was he was six months behind on his credit card payments and the credit card company had a hit man looking for him. Bruce Easily wanted to make Al Beback shit himself literally. So he called up the welfare office and impersonated Al Beback. He requested to not have any more welfare checks sent to him, as he just got hired as a high profile janitor.

"It takes talent to maintain a poker face on the phone."

—Sidney S. Prasad

TELEMARKETER'S REVENGE: THE CUSTOMER IS ALWAYS WRONG, BITCH!

UNIVERSAL LANGUAGE

I can't tell you how many times telemarketers have been lied to by a prospect claiming that they don't speak English. But it's funny that we can hear the TV or stereo blasting in the back with English lyrics or dialogue. If I were a door-to-door salesman and someone gave me that old excuse, I'd be tempted to kick the prospect in the nuts and wait for them to yell, "Ouch, you asshole!"

Perry Noid was a natural-gas sales consultant. He was combing through his database when he came across Dr. Chu's home phone number. Perry Noid lives in a small remote town and Dr. Chu has been the town's trusted dentist for many decades. Before the call, Perry Noid speculated that this would be an easy call, since he has been dealing with Dr. Chu since he was a kid. Dr. Chu answered the phone and listened to Perry Noid's spiel and then responded back in a foreign language. During the course of the call, Dr. Chu wouldn't speak a word of English, which prompted Perry Noid to ditch the call.

"Thank you for informing me that I called the wrong number, but now that I have you on the phone, how about updating our records?"

—Sidney S. Prasad

Perry Noid was really insulted after the call and knew that Dr. Chu was being coy for no apparent reason. Perry Noid thought about how much business his family had given Dr. Chu over the years and thought this would be the perfect opportunity to pay it forward. Although Perry Noid's stepmom was a hooker and didn't have any dental plan, she still supported Dr. Chu and paid in cash. Perry Noid decided he was really going to stick it to Dr. Chu.

Perry Noid called up the local paper and created an obituary for Dr. Chu to kill his business a little. Then, for the next two weeks, every night at 6:00 PM, when the dental office was closed, Perry Noid would fill the voicemail up with foreign porn vocals. Perry Noid had no remorse and just said it would have been less painful if Dr. Chu just told him flat out to fuck off.

"Some people lift weights to feel strong, while others scream at telemarketers to feel tough."

—Sidney S. Prasad

TELEMARKETER'S REVENGE: THE CUSTOMER IS ALWAYS WRONG, BITCH!

CREEPY CLIENTS

Telemarketers' ears have borne witness to the echoes of flushing toilets and people making farting sounds with their lips. They have heard every four-letter word in the dictionary and, of course, the sounds of someone screaming. However, one of the worst sounds is no sound at all. Anyone that has ever spoken to someone on the phone late at night can relate to this. Imagine looking forward all day to having sloppy phone sex with your significant other. Then, after five minutes, you don't hear anything but dead air because they got themselves off and fell asleep. Prolonged silence is one of the most disappointing things to hear for anyone, but it's worse if you work on the phone for a living.

This customer silent-treatment bullshit takes me back to one of my sales gigs in my earlier days of selling. I was required to call business-to-business selling advertising space in a local phone directory. On some occasions, I would have a dozen calls back-to-back with silence. I didn't sit on my ass and whine like a little bitch; I got even.

I didn't take it out on the prospect, but I took it out on the fucker that assigned those dead leads. I'd wait till I heard something brewing in my insides and then I'd go to my sales manager and ask a really stupid question. I would make sure the question required a long, detailed answer. As the sales manager started delivering their explanation, I'd let out a long, silent, but extremely violent fart. I kept this routine up for six months until my boss accused me of being a terrorist for dropping bombs at his desk.

"I'm sorry for interrupting you, Sir; I didn't realize it was your Internet porn night."

—Sidney S. Prasad

I'm assuming not all of my readers are talented as me and can fart on demand. But don't worry; with the right junk food combined with chili and really cheap beer, you can develop that talent as well.

The most effective way a vengeful telemarketer could get even with the client is to give the customer a taste of the same medicine. I'm talking about getting even with silent messages. All you've got to do is get one hundred envelopes with the client's address both on the front and on the back as a return address. Then, on each of the envelopes, put a one-cent stamp. Every day for the next three months, stick an envelope in the mailbox on the way to work. The envelope won't get delivered, but will get returned back to the client. The good thing about this is that you can save your breath and energy for the real assholes that piss you off on the job.

"If you believe in karma, then you shouldn't swear at strangers on the phone."

—Sidney S. Prasad

9 CURIOUS CRITTERS

Salespeople don't sell 100 percent of the time. They are human just like anyone else, and shop for groceries, tampons, and toilet paper, picking up shit they don't really need from the dollar store. Salespeople are some of the best-behaved customers when shopping. They may ask a bunch of valid questions, as they are trained to weigh out the pros and cons of the product as it usually comes up during a presentation.

Most ethical companies will train their staff to be honest with their clientele. In the event you don't know an answer, just be honest. I've had times where I've told the prospect that I'm not 100 percent sure, but let me check with the manufacturer's representative, because I would like to know that answer, too — and I absolutely get back to them. Most customers respect my honesty at that point, because they know that they are not dealing with a fly-by-night stereotypical used car salesman.

"Can a rude criminal get a pardon?"

—Sidney S. Prasad, Don't Ask Dumb Questions!

However, there are occasions when the consumer is totally out of line and unreasonable with their demands and time constraints. You can't build a house in a day, right? You can't make a pizza from scratch and have it delivered in ten minutes or less, right?

Dale E. Paper was an alarm salesman who fell victim to an unreasonable prospect. He called up Cy Yonarra one day and tried to close him on a home alarm service. Cy Yonarra was an ex-toilet salesman who knew all the quick ins and outs of escaping sales calls.

Cy Yonarra made an unusual request, stating that he would only make a buying decision provided Dale E. Paper, within the next five minutes, sent over testimonials from one hundred people who had purchased the product. Dale E. Paper was speechless, and Cy Yonarra hung up and escaped.

Now, any salesperson would agree that, due to the time constraint of five minutes, disclosing that information would be ridiculous. Dale E. Paper wanted to rub moldy peanut butter all over his balls and make Cy Yonarra lick it off. But he figured Cy Yonarra already paid his dues working a shitty job selling toilets. However, if Cy Yonarra were still was selling toilets, Dale E. Paper would be sure to take a raunchy dump in one of the showroom toilets.

TELEMARKETER'S REVENGE: THE CUSTOMER IS ALWAYS WRONG, BITCH!

Dale E. Paper managed to get the make, model, and license plate number of Cy Yonarra's car and got downright dirty. He wrote out one hundred apology letters impersonating Cy Yonarra. The apology letter included Cy Yonarra's car information and stated, "I do apologize, but I hit your car earlier today. Please contact me so we can work something out."

Then, Dale E. Paper and his telemarketing buddies sat in the parking lot of a mall, waited for some mean-looking guys to get out of their car, and stuck the note to their windshield. Let's see that fast-talking, former toilet-bowl salesman get out of this shitty situation.

"Sorry, I don't live here, I just answer the phones."

—Sidney S. Prasad

TIME IS MONEY

As expressed earlier, regardless of occupation, time is money. A business guru in a seminar once preached that in order for an entity to be profitable, the employee must yield a minimum of five times their wage in productivity or sales. A simple sandwich artist can't sit and chat for an hour about their latest breakthrough in combining salad dressing and mustard to the customers. A cashier shouldn't take two hours to ring up a customer or half the line will walk out. My patience wouldn't allow me to wait three hours for someone to wax my back unless they were using their teeth. The sad thing is, some people have all the time in the world and don't mind taking twenty minutes to wipe their ass.

Chris Mass was employed for a firm that specialized in pet insurance, a nifty New Age concept that comes in handy for pet owners. One day, she called upon Constance Paine and enlightened her about their service. Constance Paine was a real pain in the derrière. She started bitching about the malfunctioning elastic in her underpants, and then ranted about her personal baggage for the next hour and a half. She even disclosed that her boyfriend only slept with her on paydays. Chris Mass eventually had to email her boss during the call to get the O.K. to hang up.

TELEMARKETER'S REVENGE: THE CUSTOMER IS ALWAYS WRONG, BITCH!

"Telemarketers are life-savers; They always call at the right time to remind me that dinner is about to be served."

—Sidney S. Prasad

Although Chris Mass did the right thing in getting her boss's permission to hang up on that Needy Nelly, she still got in bucket loads of shit for wasting that hour and a half. Chris Mass was paranoid her boss was going to take her fringe benefits away. (The fringe benefits consisted of unlimited use of an outhouse and eight-track-cassette borrowing privileges.) Chris Mass pictured herself hiding outside Constance Paine's window with a universal remote control and constantly changing her TV channels until she went crazy. Bad idea, because Constance Paine might call her back and whine about it.

Chris Mass got the ultimate telemarketer's revenge by opening up an email account under Constance Paine's name. Here's the kicker: She emailed Constance Paine's boss pretending to be her, called him every name in the book, and then resigned.

CAN'T HEAR YOU

I can appreciate that in the age of information technology, a large percentage of people have switched to digital newspapers and magazine subscriptions. I'm pretty old-fashioned myself and prefer to borrow the newspaper from the doughnut shop or the library newspaper that comes with the free backscratcher stick. But whether a prospect has completely opted out of using hard-copy magazines and newspapers or uses a combination of digital and hard copy, they should have some respect for the person trying to offer them a good old-fashioned piece of literature. If a prospect doesn't read avidly, they should be upfront and just disclose that between the shampoo bottle and mouthwash jug in their shitter, that's enough reading material for the next year.

Holly Wood worked at a publishing house that distributed a foreign mail-order bride magazine subscription. She called up and approached Dan Druff one afternoon in hopes of securing a one-year subscription with him. It was blatantly obvious that Dan Druff was taking a dump during the call because she could hear the echoes of something solid hitting the water. Holly Wood wasn't used to dealing with sick fucks like Dan Druff who take their phone in the shitter with them and actually answer it. She'd understand if it were a security blanket thing, but to actually talk on it while it's sitting next to your toilet? Eww, gross!

TELEMARKETER'S REVENGE: THE CUSTOMER IS ALWAYS WRONG, BITCH!

"Who is paying you to harass me? I will double whatever they're paying you for you to solicit them during the playoffs."

—Sidney S. Prasad

Dan Druff was an expert with dealing with people while on the throne. He knew if he opened his mouth and attempted to speak normally, he would sound like a girl, as half his concentration was on releasing some missiles into the toilet. So he thought he'd handle the situation in a passive-aggressive manner. Every time Holly Wood would ask Dan Druff a question, he would answer back, whispering. After about five minutes of going nowhere with Dan Druff, Holly Wood gave up and let him take his shit in peace.

Holly Wood originally wanted to lock Dan Druff in his washroom and seal the windows shut, forcing him to smell his own shit for two hours. "But he's probably immune to the smell by now," she thought. Then, she thought about getting every telemarketer in the firm to call him continuously and make him lose his concentration on the shitter, causing him to fall in the toilet. But he is probably a strong swimmer, since he lives so close to the ocean.

During Holly Wood's lunch break, she got her boyfriend to call up the electric company and impersonate Dan Druff. Her boyfriend said that he was moving and to turn off the electricity immediately, because he wasn't going to pay for it after tomorrow.

"If I wanted someone to ask me how I'm feeling, then I would go see my doctor!"

—Sidney S. Prasad

WHO GIVES A SHIT?

Nothing happens in life until someone makes a fucken' sale. Take a look at the leading fast-food restaurants of America. If there weren't pimple-faced, bifocal-wearing, sweaty cashiers pushing burgers and French fries down the customers' throats, then they wouldn't have a need to replenish their inventory and order more sawdust-filled burgers and potatoes, which would mean the farmers and roadkill burger salesmen would have no jobs, leaving the shareholders with a dying stock. The same school of thought can be applied to almost any large long-distance carrier. They wouldn't exist if it weren't for the brilliant telemarketers that call you during dinner.

Once in a while, when a telemarketer calls up the odd prospect, they might not sound like a stewardess making an announcement on a one-hour flight. How good would you sound after listening to customers and their children telling you to fuck off for eight hours working in a boiler room?

Nidda Betajob was a cold caller for a home insurance company. She called up Lee Vemealowne, but was a little out of breath because she just finished having sex with her boss in the broom closet.

TELEMARKETER'S REVENGE: THE CUSTOMER IS ALWAYS WRONG, BITCH!

"Essentially, everything in life is a sale, whether it's pitching prospects, selling yourself to a potential employer, or convincing your girlfriend which drive-thru to have your anniversary dinner at."

—Sidney S. Prasad

Lee Vemealowne questioned her immediately and asked her why she was out of breath. He then called her a phone hooker and accused her of touching herself on the job. She's like, "I used to do that on my old job, but state regulation doesn't allow phone sex operators in this county." (But really, who cares if she was out of breath as long as she can convey her sales pitch, right?) Lee Vemealowne said, "I'm going to do you a favor and let you continue treating your body like a smorgasbord" and hung up.

Nidda Betajob knew she had to make an example out of this asshole and eat his lunch for him. Now, she could mail him some used condoms and tampons or vomit, but that still wouldn't be enough restitution for what he said. She could order twenty pizzas from twenty different pizza parlors and send them to his address. But he might be a fat fuck and actually eat all of it. She decided to terrorize the fuck head and really make him pay with a care package.

She went to the library and cut out a bunch of news articles about unsolved hate crimes, home invasions, and manslaughters and inserted them into a box. She then added a couple of bullets and an axe, accompanied by a skull she purchased from the joke store, and combined it with the news articles and left it on his doorstep. It could have been worse if she burnt a dozen phones on his lawn. But telemarketers aren't that psycho… I think.

"Excuse me. You got me confused with someone that gives a shit!"

—Sidney S. Prasad

10 COME IN AND SHIT DOWN

It's sort of ironic. Nowadays, everyone carries a camera with them, or at least on their cell phone. You can purchase home surveillance and check on your house from any computer in the world. With all this in mind, you have to wonder why crime is at a record high.

During the real estate boom in the last decade, people would purposely target realtors and sellers. In some cases, the realtor was held at gunpoint by clients and made to give up his wallet and jewelry. But the one that just sickened me was the knowledge that there are people who pose as couples and meet a realtor to view houses. One person would distract the realtor, while the other rummaged through the drawers and stole whatever they could get their hands on.

Some people are blessed with having great friends that they unconditionally trust, while others may have friends but not be sure if they can trust them or not. With this in mind, there is a market for house-sitting. Sure, it sounds strange to have a stranger minding your house, but for someone like Phyllis Teen, who is employed at a company that fully screened her, it's not that much of a risk, right?

"Actions speak louder than words. That's why I'm slamming the phone on your ass!"

—Sidney S. Prasad

Phyllis Teen made a cold call to Willie B. Long to see if the Willster would be interested in house-sitting services. Willie B. Long blew a gasket and unloaded a can of whoop-ass on Phyllis Teen. His response was, "Excuse me, are you retarded and mentally unstable? I don't want no stranger to eat my shit, sleep on my shit, and shit on my fucken' toilet!" He then hung up on her.

Phyllis Teen was astonished by Willie B. Long's response. Personally, she wanted to shit on a plate and throw it in his microwave for twenty minutes. But, she figured he would probably enjoy that kind of freaky shit. Then, she thought about putting some razor blades in his sofa cushions and imagined him screaming at the top of his lungs. But she was single-handed and would need more help to get even with this fucker.

While brainstorming revenge tactics, she noticed in the paper that a well-known controversial religious cult was having a rally at a community park the following day. So Phyllis Teen went to the toy store, purchased a remote-control airplane, and wrote Willie B. Long's name, phone number, and address on it. She purposely crashed the plane at the rally.

"Since you know where I live, why don't you come over so I can shove my energy bill up your ass!"

—Sidney S. Prasad

TELEMARKETER'S REVENGE: THE CUSTOMER IS ALWAYS WRONG, BITCH!

I'LL BE BACK!

Readers, by this point in the book I'm pretty confident you can agree that the customer is always wrong! Not only is the customer always wrong, but the customer is usually dumb… at least the ones mentioned in this book so far.

Businesses pay a hefty sum of money in purchasing prospect leads. They aren't simply going to burn the leads because some customer was having a bad day and said they weren't interested in being sold to. Customers really need to wake up and smell the free refill coffee and learn to how to deal with telemarketers. Hanging up on a salesperson almost guarantees a callback in the future. Saying one is busy will also result in a callback. This isn't rocket science, right?

Barb E. Cue was in the business of selling and promoting refurbished toilet seats. She came across Al Coholic's phone number and thought she might try her luck at selling him a reconditioned shitter seat. Al Coholic listened to Barb E. Cue's pitch and then used his cell phone to interrupt his landline call with Barb E. Cue. He said, "Hold on, there's another call," and he never returned.

Now, I don't know if Al Coholic was already drinking or smoking a funny cigarette or something as he got her off the hook for that moment. But this call would be normally thrown right back in the callback section of the database.

"Would you take it personally if I told you to fuck off?"

—Sidney S. Prasad

Barb E. Cue had her own special way of dealing with difficult personality types like Al Coholic, so she immediately rescheduled a callback for five minutes after he hung up. She also put a second rescheduled callback for fifteen minutes from that call, and another one for half an hour after the third call. (Sometimes it's funny when the tables are turned and you work in a big enough call center to get away with it.)

To make his life even more complicated, she sold his number to a couple of calling lists in India and Hong Kong. Now he will have to deal with telemarketers with funny accents in the middle of the night, as well.

"If you are busy, then why didn't you leave the phone off the hook?"

—Sidney S. Prasad

TELEMARKETER'S REVENGE: THE CUSTOMER IS ALWAYS WRONG, BITCH!

UNREASONABLE

With the combination of my colleagues' experience and my personal expertise being employed in the field of kissing the customer's ass, we all hypothesize the same thing. Society has a false perception that salespeople and customer service officials have all the fucken' time in the world to pamper consumers. It's sort of like they think companies can manage to stay afloat by having one person stay on the phone for hours handling one consumer's petty wishes. Believe it or not, most salespeople have a quota for how many people they contact, both incoming and outgoing calls. I remember a decade ago, I was hooked up to a instant dialer and I'd be on the hook for contacting roughly four hundred people per shift, which included answering machines, hang-ups, quick one-second fuck-offs, ten-second go-fuck-yourselfs and maybe fifty live conversations.

The point I'm trying to emphasize is that even though our customer bum-licking occupations aren't that glamorous, we are busy, too. Fuck, there are even computer-generated reports now that rat out call center employees — the reports measure the lengths of the calls.

Pee Don Yu was a telemarketer who promoted the services for pest control and pest extermination. He called up Anne Chovie one night trying to drum up some business. Anne Chovie requested a two-for-one special, because she claimed her husband had more crabs than a seafood platter. Pee Don Yu explained that they specialized in pest control services, and she would have to see a pharmacist regarding her husband's pubic lice.

"You're calling me from work? Well, then give me your home number and I'll call you tomorrow from work."

—Sidney S. Prasad

Anne Chovie said that she would have to think about the proposition while she took a shit. She estimated it was going to be at least forty-five minutes because she was exterminating some chili dogs and poutine. Pee Don Yu offered a callback in forty-five minutes, and Anne Chovie said the only way she would consider making a deal is if Pee Don Yu stayed on the line and listened to her shit for forty-five minutes. Pee Don Yu made a split-second decision and hit the "off" button on the power strip that was powering his entire computer and phone. (By the way, a lot of veteran telemarketers use this as an escape to get out of listening to someone take a dump.)

TELEMARKETER'S REVENGE: THE CUSTOMER IS ALWAYS WRONG, BITCH!

Now you can't blame Pee Don Yu for being pissed at this bitch. His original plan to get even was to take a bag of dog shit to Anne Chovie's doorstep and light it on fire, then run like a little bitch. But he figured she'd enjoy stomping on the bag of burning doggie doo.

Pee Don Yu was the quiet type and sort of a psycho. He decided to stalk Anne Chovie for a week to figure out what car she drove and when she and her husband went to sleep. Then, at the beginning of the second week, he jimmied open her car, put a pair of men's underwear with a big shit stain on it and a box of condoms in the back seat. He also rinsed two condoms with milk and left them on the floor. Pee Don Yu felt the punishment was suitable for the crime.

"Just to make it fair, please tell me your name, number, and where you live before I answer your questions."

—Sidney S. Prasad

BUCK NUDE

Is society getting sicker, or has the mainstream media been hiding it from us the whole time? It seems people are getting more scandalous as we transcend into the twenty-first century. People walk around half-naked today, wearing almost nothing when half a century ago, the norm for dresses was three inches below the knees. Plus, all the different fetishes people are confessing to having, ranging from being obsessed with pooh to eating dessert off their partners' bodies. I can only speculate that there are more nudist camps today than a decade ago. But I guess that is the beauty of living in a democratic society: being allowed to do almost anything that comes to mind within certain parameters.

Mack Aroni was an inside sales representative for a company that sold vacuums. One day, he phoned Neil Downe in hopes of arranging an in-home vacuum demonstration. Initially, Neil Downe appeared to be genuinely interested in the product. Then, out of nowhere, like an old man who had too much prune juice with his sardine sandwich, he dropped a bomb. Neil Downe had the audacity to ask Mack Aroni what he was wearing.

Mack Aroni went both ways and really didn't mind some friendly flirting if that's what it took to get the sale. So Mack Aroni told Neil Downe that he was wearing some leather pants with the butt cheeks cut out and a policeman-style hat with gold studs. Neil Downe said, "Guess what I'm wearing? Nothing. I'm buck nude."

TELEMARKETER'S REVENGE: THE CUSTOMER IS ALWAYS WRONG, BITCH!

"Sorry, I don't talk to strange people that work in boiler rooms!"

—Sidney S. Prasad

Most salespeople at this point would have hung up and resigned from their two-figure telemarketing job. But I have to hand it to Mack Aroni; he was a trouper and hung in there. Mack Aroni empathetically said he'd prefer to be nude, too, with the heat wave they'd recently encountered. Neil Downe then requested that Mack Aroni take all his clothes off and prove it with a picture, and then he would agree to have a vacuum demonstration. Mack Aroni would gladly scan his bare ass and email it to Neil Downe, but getting buck nude at the workplace is going a little too far.

Mack Aroni knew at this point that he wouldn't get fired if he ended the call due to the circumstances. So he asked Neil Downe to hold on and then called his sales manager. He then told his sales manager that her husband was on the line, and then took his lunch break.

During Mack Aroni's break, he brainstormed on how he could get even with this sick fuck. He thought about installing a reverse peephole on Neil Downe's door, but then the poor mailman would see his bits and pieces. Mack Aroni took a quick drive by Neil Downe's house and noticed a brand new car in the driveway with a license-plate holder advertising the local dealer that he purchased it from. Mack Aroni then got one of his friends to call Neil Downe and impersonate the car dealer, saying that there was a recall on his car. He instructed Neil Downe not to drive it under any circumstances, as the results could be deadly, and wait until they could send a tow truck next week to pick up his vehicle.

"You didn't call a candy store and I'm not a sucker."

—Sidney S. Prasad

TELEMARKETER'S REVENGE: THE CUSTOMER IS ALWAYS WRONG, BITCH!

In conclusion, I ask you: What would be the ultimate revenge to get even with those bonehead prospects? I ask myself that question every time someone hangs up on me or tells me to go have sex with myself. I sometimes fantasize about a whole call center full of telemarketers calling someone up every two minutes, 24/7, until they either go crazy and check into the nuthouse or change their number.

I really wonder how the prospect would react if the salesperson announced that the prospect's four-letter words motivated them to quit their job on the spot, and that now they are on their way to the prospect's house to speak, face to face. It's scary to imagine what would happen if the prospect opened his door to discover a maniac with a headset on his head and a phone cord in his hands, ready to strangle someone. With the amount of abuse and bullying telemarketers take, it wouldn't surprise me if this has already been done, or will happen one day.

It wouldn't be astonishing to pick up a newspaper or hear a story one day on the nightly news about a telemarketer jumping off the call-center roof. If the average person read the same script five thousand times, they would go insane, too. Between the repetition of our scripts and the customer bullshit, something's got to give, right?

"The beauty of selling long-distance plans is you never run out of product."

—Sidney S. Prasad

I'm not trying to say that all consumers are wrong, as there are those rare individuals who welcome telemarketing calls and actually purchase our products and services. But I'm trying to make an example out of those punks that purposely wait for a sales call to dump all over the representative. Or those individuals who play their snarly little games and use lame-ass excuses.

Throughout this book, we covered typical roommate pranks and outrageously demented pranks. But there is one prank that would make the history books and land the telemarketer in jail for the next twenty years that I never mentioned. I can only imagine this being executed on the big screen, but I can visualize a telemarketer losing it and arranging for the prospect's house to get bulldozed. Consumers would think twice before messing with a telemarketer if someone ever pulled it off.

In a fantasy world, there are a million things a telemarketer can do to get their revenge on the customer, ranging from dumping maggots on the prospect's doorstep to pissing on their barbecue or making a B.S. complaint to the authorities. But in reality, the telemarketer would be stooping to the prospect's level and could lose their job, end up in jail, or feel really shitty for two minutes for doing something cruel.

TELEMARKETER'S REVENGE: THE CUSTOMER IS ALWAYS WRONG, BITCH!

"Quit calling me. You're beginning to remind me of my girlfriend!"

—Sidney S. Prasad

As mentioned a few times in this book, I wrote this for pure entertainment for my colleagues who serve the public for a living. We all have a prankster living inside us, dying to come out once in a while, but we are bounded by the laws of karma. For every action, there is a reaction, some may believe. So even if you think you can get away with it, in a metaphysical sense someone is always watching, and you can never go against the universe.

For what it's worth, if someone were to ask me what I personally think would be the best revenge on a crappy prospect, it is very simple: Grab a headset and make them be a telemarketer for a day. Most average people would quit by the first coffee break, as they would be overwhelmed with the kind of funky shit that we encounter on a typical day. Or worse, they would be preaching that "The Customer Is Always Wrong, Bitch," and then get their revenge!

"The customer is always right, except when they say, 'don't call back!'"

—Sidney S. Prasad

ABOUT THE AUTHOR

Sidney S. Prasad is an author on a quest to make the world laugh. His work is focused on entertaining people with his dry-humored novels. Sidney S. Prasad personally believes laughter is the best cure for all of life's ups and downs.

Some other humorous books written by Sidney S. Prasad include:

How To Piss Off A Telemarketer,
My Bipolar Manager,
Don't Ask Dumb Questions!,
My Stupid CEO,
Plenty Of Freaks: Are You Sold On Online Dating?
Plenty Of Freaks: Worst Online Dating Mistakes
and
Corny Names & Stupid Places

www.ingramcontent.com/pod-product-compliance
Lightning Source LLC
Chambersburg PA
CBHW071956070426
42453CB00008BA/805